The Student Journalist
and
LEGAL AND ETHICAL ISSUES

THE STUDENT JOURNALIST AND

PRESS TIME—The moment the first issue comes off the press, students check for errors before distributing the newspaper. Photograph by San Bernardino Sun-Telegram.

THE
STUDENT
JOURNALIST
GUIDE
SERIES

LEGAL AND ETHICAL ISSUES

by

SAMUEL N. FELDMAN

PUBLISHED BY
RICHARDS ROSEN
PRESS, INC.
NEW YORK

Library of Congress Catalog Card Number: 68-16623

Published in 1968 by Richards Rosen Press, Inc.
29 East 21st Street, New York City, N.Y. 10010

Manufactured in the United States of America

Revised Edition

To Arleigh McConnell, Mabel A. Stanford, Roy L. French, Christina D. Beeson, and the late Wilbur Mackcy: they knew the difference between right and wrong—and how to report it.

When he was editor of his seventh-grade newspaper, young Sam Feldman predicted he would become a writer. And for the past twenty-five years he has been active as a newspaperman, teacher, and consultant. Although he was born in Brooklyn, Feldman has lived in California for nearly three decades. Attending Chaffey High School in Ontario, California, he was editor of both the newspaper and the yearbook. In junior college he was also editor of the newspaper, and he majored in journalism at the University of Southern California.

Starting his career as a copy boy for the *Los Angeles Daily News,* he became a reporter and sports editor for the *Fontana Herald-News* and night sports editor for the *San Bernardino Sun-Telegram.* In addition, he was co-publisher and co-editor of a small weekly on outdoor sports. While he was adviser to the newspaper and yearbook at San Bernardino High School, his students won several major newspaper awards for excellence, including one at his alma mater, the University of Southern California. Among his innovations as a teacher were the use of newsmagazine format and plastic engravings and the establishment of junior-high journalism day. After six years in the classroom, he joined the San Bernardino County Schools Office in 1963 as English and journalism consultant.

It was as a teacher that he became concerned with the legal and ethical issues of student journalism, and his master's degree subject at the University of Redlands was on the legal aspects. He is currently working toward a doctorate at the University of California at Los Angeles.

Among extracurricular activities, he was charter president of the Inland Chapter of Sigma Delta Chi, the national journalistic society, president of the area Journalism Education Association, and a Newspaper Fund Fellow. As a writer he won the 1964

Associated Press regional first-place award in sports writing and more than a score of awards in the Twin Counties Press Club contests.

A onetime semi-pro baseball player, Feldman still retains an active interest in sports, which he combines with his favorite hobby, chess.

CONTENTS

PREFACE

"What would you do if I told you not to print a story?" the high-school principal asked.

The teacher candidate hesitated only slightly.

"If your reasons were sound, I wouldn't print it. If it happened too often, I'd look for another school."

Suddenly I began to realize that after a decade of being a student editor and professional reporter, I had no one to "pass the buck to." There had always been an understanding teacher or a veteran copy editor to consult, but now I would have to serve as adviser to a group of turned-on teen-agers. I knew the mechanics of journalism, but I needed a guide to the legal and ethical limits of the high-school press. I couldn't find one. A decade later I still find there is a need for such a guide. Yet this book is not meant to be just a "vehicle code" for the legal-minded teacher and student. Cases are cited—the few that I could find. If you know of others, write the publisher so that I may include them in a future revision. The real purpose of the book is to encourage the timid and caution the careless.

After more than two decades in journalism at various levels, I must confess there are fewer restrictions on scholastic news-papers than on professional newspapers. Principals usually have fewer "sacred cows" than publishers, and less pressure from advertisers. The dilemma of student journalism is that the public judges you by professional standards, yet at the same time you must teach a class and allow students the same chance to make mistakes that they need in any regular class. We often learn most from our failures. The student who misspells a faculty name learns that it is far different from misspelling a name on an essay read only by the teacher. There are no set answers to many of the problems posed in the book. Each community, each school, and each class causes you to react differently. In one week the high-school principal acted as host to Dr. James Conant and was hanged in effigy. The newspaper printed both pictures. This type of objectivity is perhaps the most difficult quality to teach—not only to students, but to teachers and parents. Principals should realize this, but the majority do not. The proudest day a teacher can have is the one when he realizes the staff can function and make difficult decisions by themselves. This is one of the major objectives of journalism, pushing the student out on the editorial limb and waiting to see if he will fly or saw the limb off.

Many acknowledgments are in order. First, to publishers for permission to reprint cases and stories. To others, such as Bill Ward for encouragement and Dr. Ken Devol for material. Three friends read the manuscript and made suggestions—teacher Chris Beeson, newspaperman Jim McKone, and attorney Ed Taylor. Librarians—particularly Dora Buzzi—helped me track down material.

The book was designed to keep the student journalist out of court and out of the principal's office. I hope it does both.

SAMUEL N. FELDMAN

The Student Journalist
and
LEGAL AND ETHICAL ISSUES

Chapter 1

INTRODUCTION

> *How vain it is to sit*
> *down to write when you*
> *have not stood up to live.*
> —HENRY DAVID THOREAU

A high-school senior in New York filed a $1,000,000 libel suit because of a caption in her high school yearbook.

The adviser of a California junior-college magazine lost a $180,000 libel suit against a weekly publisher who called the student magazine pornographic.

Editors of five high-school underground newspapers around Los Angeles cited censorship, administrative paternalism, and lack of freedom among the reasons for their existence.

Do these recent cases signal a coming crisis in the student press comparable to the controversy that continues among college newspapers? What are the legal and ethical issues currently facing junior-high, high-school, and junior-college journalists?

Although disputes over student publications have been increasing in frequency during the past few years, the fact that nearly all scholastic libel cases have been settled out of court has tended to create a myth that schools are virtually immune to such court action.

The purpose of this book is to make the student and teacher aware of both the legal and ethical responsibilities inherent in scholastic journalism.

This is not a libel textbook. The problem is to discover whether and how press law applies to student journalism. Much

15

COVERAGE PROBLEM—High-school students covering such off-campus protests are sometimes criticized by school officials for becoming involved. Photograph by Blair Breeze.

has been written for the college journalist, but editors and advisers of an estimated 100,000 publications in grades 9 through 14 have virtually no guide in deciding what to print.

College journalism recently made the headlines again when a student editor in Oregon refused to reveal her news source in a story on drugs. Professionals leaped to her aid, claiming that this right extends to the campus, and helped to raise legal fees to fight the contempt citation by the court.

Yearbooks have also made the headlines. In Florida, when a comely college yearbook editor used nearly two dozen pictures of herself in the publication, the students protested by destroying copies of the book. The young woman maintained that the coverage was not excessive, since she had been selected campus queen and was active in numerous clubs.

Whether the First Amendment guarantee of freedom of the press extends to the public schools is still a moot point, but an interpretation may be forthcoming in the next decade.

THE NEW JOURNALISM

The cries of Student Power from the college students, Black Power from the Negroes, and Flower Power from the hippies may soon cause secondary-school journalists to demand Press Power. The flourishing underground press in the high schools may be more than just another teen-age fad.

If the so-called generation gap continues, students may distrust anyone over twenty-one instead of the stated thirty of today. This means that teachers may have increasing difficulty preventing militant student journalists from printing off campus what they cannot print on campus.

Hippies, Black Muslims and numerous schools have already "turned off" the established media to create their own publications. The college and professional journalists are debating whether education should consist of practical courses in writing and editing or should stress communications research. The newspapers want to stress the practical, but the professors feel that communication theory should be part of the well-balanced curriculum. This dilemma should also be considered by the second-ary-school adviser. Does a production class justify the awarding of credit in journalism, or should the student study mass media and communications? Is the beginning journalism course too re-stricted in favor of newspapers? What about television, maga-zines, movies, advertising, propaganda, public relations, pub-licity?

The Journalism Education Association is preparing the New Journalism that will be placed in the curriculum alongside the New Math, New Biology, and New English. The media war be-tween newspapers and television may be reflected here. Roper Polls from 1959 to 1967 reveal that television has risen from 42 to 53 percent as the most favored medium, while newspapers have declined from 32 to 26 percent.

Current innovations in education may force us to revise courses such as journalism, which fall somewhere between ex-tracurricular and academic in the curriculum spectrum. Inquiry training and the inductive method that go along with the content revisions may force teachers away from the authoritative ap-proach and students into learning to ask more and better ques-tions to arrive at their own conclusions. Learning is said to be more meaningful with this method, and the student newspaper may also have to reflect the more thoughtful atmosphere in the school.

The student-body president of a large high school in West Los Angeles was suspended in June 1967, after criticizing the principal in his farewell address. How would your school news-paper have covered the story? The *Los Angeles Times* carried a major story and picture on the suspension and the subsequent student strike, and a follow-up story when the president was allowed to return to school.

PUBLICATION CODES

Such fads as miniskirts for the girls and long hair for the boys have provided the aggressive student press in junior highs and high schools with something more than clean campus and school spirit as editorial topics. When commercial television covers such controversies, the exposure is almost too much for the harassed school administrator. Too many administrators fail to see the need for adequate dress codes until they have to react under pressure to a crisis. The same may be said concerning publications codes. The machinery to handle controversial subjects should be ready before, rather than after, they spring up. A meeting early in the year among publication staffs, student leaders, and administrators to discuss specific guides as to what should and will be published could prevent future difficulties. At least they will not arise because of ignorance or misunderstanding, and when they do come up, each side will be prepared to settle them properly.

Disputes are not easily settled, as the Manchester-Kennedy battle over the editing of *Death of a President* will attest. It is an example of how involved editorial arrangements can become even when just one writer is concerned.

The furor over the Warren Commission Report demonstrates that an entire nation cannot decide without some doubts as to the reporting of one of the most important stories of the century. The errors of omission as well as commission during even such extensive reporting by the mass media illustrate the dangers of publishing. The Warren Commission chastised the press and TV for their coverage of the assassination; yet it should be pointed out that such instant disclosure of the event helped calm an almost hysterical nation during a crisis.

The Supreme Court has probably tempered sports writing by its recent ruling upholding a $460,000 libel judgment against *The Saturday Evening Post* by former University of Georgia football coach Wally Butts.

Before looking at some cases and issues in the student press, let us define some basic terms that will be helpful to you.

TERMINOLOGY

(1) School publications: Newspapers, yearbooks, and magazines published in grades 9 through 14.

(2) Libel: Printed defamation holding a person up to hatred, ridicule, or contempt.

(3) Privilege: Absolute or qualified immunity from libel through publication of legislative, judicial, or public news.

(4) Privacy: Right of every man to live his life free from unsolicited publicity, yet subject to the rights of others.

(5) a. Character: What a man is.

b. Reputation: What his fellow men think he is.

(6) Malice: Motive of personal spite or ill will toward an individual.

(7) Fair comment: An honest opinion that does not impugn a person's integrity or motives, but comments on the work or act itself.

(8) Libel per se: Words that need no explanation in order to determine their defamatory effect.

(9) Libel per quod: Words not actionable in themselves, but libelous when special damages are proved.

(10) Nol-pros (*nolle prosequi*): To be unwilling to prosecute.

(11) Tort: A civil wrong for which the remedy is an action for damages.

(12) General damages: Damages for loss of reputation, shame, mortification, and hurt feelings.

(13) Special damages: Damages that the plaintiff alleges and proves he has suffered in respect to his property, business, trade, profession, or occupation, including such amounts of money expended as a result of the libel.

(14) Punitive or exemplary damages: Damages that may, in the discretion of the court or jury, be recovered in addition to genēral and special damages for the sake of example and by way of punishing a defendant for malice.

(15) In loco parentis: In place of the parent.

Chapter 2

CASES

The truth that makes men free
is very often the truth they
do not like to hear.
—JAMES RESTON

Because scholastic publications have a tendency to libel friends rather than enemies, few cases have been taken to court. Two cases to be cited occurred within months of each other although 3,000 miles apart. The first demonstrates that a publication jests at its own peril. The law has no humor. This type of misapprehension is also a high-school problem. The second case reveals that junior-college students are becoming more sophisticated in politics and satire. Perhaps there is a gap between what a community regards as acceptable journalism and what the academic world believes is critical writing. The two cases show that the latitude of public tolerance is decreasing.

THE BICKERTON CASE

One of the difficulties with a pending case is that neither party will comment on it. The $1,000,000 suit brought by Irene Bickerton against Central High School in Merrick, Long Island, because of a caption in the school yearbook could become a key case in scholastic journalism. Neither party will answer questions about the case, which was filed in 1962 and subsequently settled out of court. A court ruling could have set a precedent throughout the nation. Such cases usually are settled out of court, which is the major reason why there is a dearth of rulings on scholastic libel.

21

Yet the Bickerton case, as reported in *The New York Times,* is almost typical of high-school journalism problems:

MINEOLA, L.I.—Sept. 25—A $1,000,000 libel suit was filed in State Supreme Court here today on behalf of a 16-year-old former high-school student who was allegedly ridiculed in her high-school yearbook.

The suit charges that a caption under a photograph of Irene Bickerton in the 1962 Pacer, the yearbook of the Sanford H. Calhoun High School in Merrick, was a false, scandalous, and defamatory statement.

The caption on Page 103 of the yearbook, which was distributed to the graduating class about June 12, said:

> A soft, meek, patient, humble, tranquil spirit . . .
> Thomas Dekker—"The Honest Whore."

The line was from Part I, Act I, Scene II of the Dekker play, written in 1604. He introduced it as an epitomization of a gentleman.

The suit alleges that in the yearbook caption the meanings specifically intended to be conveyed were vicious, insidious, and calculated to injure and were the meanings which naturally would be given . . . and were given by persons who read them.

The defendants in the suit are the Board of Education of Central High School District 3; Anthony W. Yenerallo, principal of Calhoun High School, and the American Yearbook Company, the publisher.

Miss Bickerton is seeking damages of $750,000; her mother $40,-000; her stepfather, $140,000; and seven other members of her family, $10,000 each. . . .

Melvyn Altman of Germaise, Freitag & Altman, the law firm representing the plaintiffs, said about 500 copies of the yearbook had been distributed. According to a member of the school board, about half of the books were recalled and the caption was changed to: "Gentle of speech, beneficent of mind"—Homer, "Odyssey."

THE PALOMAR CASE

Near San Diego, a small, conservative weekly newspaper, published by William K. Shearer, attacked an issue of the Palomar Junior College *Focus* magazine as pornographic. The June 21, 1962, editorial in the *San Marcos News-Advertiser* touched off a $180,000 libel suit against Shearer by Richard S. Johnson, Palomar journalism teacher and adviser to the magazine. The suit charged that Shearer's editorial attack damaged Johnson personally and professionally.

Some of the comments Shearer made in the June 21 editorial are as follows:

One of the most degrading pieces of publicly provided pornography known to this paper has just come down the walk under college sponsorship. . . . *Focus* is 36 pages of pointlessness interspersed with lewdness and bad thinking. What kind of adult editorial board approved this product is beyond our comprehension. . . . Politically, the magazine *Focus* bears due left. . . . It is a combination of pornography, left-wing political theories, bad taste, senselessness, and distorted history. Most students will want to hide it from their children, not show it to them. . . . Nothing but a monkey would want to read *Focus* and this paper seriously doubts that the Palomar magazine would do anything to uplift baboons or any other creature now known to mankind. Meanwhile, taxpayers, you paid for it. How do you like what your taxes bought at Palomar?

The *San Diego Evening Tribune* covered the trial extensively during August 1963. Although not a party to the suit, Dr. John W. Dunn, Palomar president, backed Johnson fully. Dunn mailed copies of the controversial magazine to thirty-five literary critics and professors of English at universities throughout the country. All of the replies felt that the magazine was representative of college thought. Johnson's fellow professors aided him financially in his fight and also testified in his behalf. Two newspapers, the *Oceanside Blade-Tribune* and the *Escondido Times-Advocate,* also backed the magazine and Johnson against Shearer's charges.

The Palomar College Board of Trustees, by a 3–1 vote, issued the following statement on July 2, 1962:

In the light of criticism of the Associated Student Body publication *Focus,* the following statement is made by the Board of Governors of Palomar College.

1. As in modern art, literature is subject to interpretation, and interpretation will vary according to the perception of the holder.
   a. Reactions to *Focus* have been many and varied.
   b. Many have been enthusiastic about the evidence of talent among contributors to the publication.
   c. Favorable comments have been received from a number of university authorities and officials.
   d. Attorneys have read the issue and one commented, "The only reason it is not in *The New Yorker* is that it is not quite good enough."
   e. The evaluation of the County Grand Jury does not reflect the opinion of this Board.
2. Academic affairs can only be conducted in an atmosphere of freedom.
   a. All who would exercise freedom must realize the accompanying requirements of responsibility.
   b. If a choice must be made between censorship and freedom with an occasional error, the choice must still be with freedom. Students learn from errors as well as from successes.
   c. Such attacks as that which prompts this statement must be classified with recent attempts to remove books from school libraries, and in other ways exercise thought control.
3. The Board of Governors of Palomar College reaffirms its policy with regard to student publications.
   a. The basic American tradition of freedom of the press must be preserved in the educational program as well as in society as a whole.
   b. The Board expects the administration to continue its efforts to guide students in the full acceptance of the responsibility which must accompany freedom, and to encourage free expression within the framework of responsibility.
   c. The Board further requests that an outline of the student publication program for the year 1962–63 be presented to the Board at the first meeting of September 1962.

One of the key witnesses for Shearer was Albert M. Wright, of La Jolla, a retired Navy commander who was foreman of the 1962 San Diego County Grand Jury.

Wright testified that he thought the magazine was "inimical to good morals, to honest religious beliefs, and to the American form of government. I was shocked and surprised that this type of literature was put out for teen-agers at Palomar College. A large part of it bordered on the pornographic. It was antireligious at times, and I thought it covered things not in the best interests of the United States." [1]

Two of the disputed points covered Indians in early California and the McCarran Act. Johnson's attorney, James L. Kintz, produced a history book, published in 1922, that said that Indians in the missions had been enslaved and mistreated. Kintz also showed that President Harry S Truman had vetoed the McCarran anti-Communist bill on September 22, 1949. Wright had objected to stories in the magazine that had made these two points, on the grounds that the comments were antireligious and un-American.

The Superior Court jury took only two hours to clear Shearer of the libel charge. The vote was 10–2; a majority, not a unanimous, vote is all that is necessary in a civil action of this kind. Johnson decided not to appeal the verdict because of financial and personal reasons:

"The expense of the trial was great and the mental strain over the past year for me and my family has been such that I have decided not to continue the case. The difficulty in finding a suitable jury was one of the factors in the vote. Only one person on the jury had a college education. The anti-intellectual climate and the extreme conservatism in the area were other factors. We felt the case was presented properly. The attorney was objective and thorough. Expert witnesses in college publications backed us completely. The jury obviously did not have the exposure and background necessary to judge itself and it evidently didn't agree with the professors who testified," Johnson said after the verdict.

The court, in essence, backed Shearer's charge of pornog-

---

[1] News item in the *San Diego Evening Tribune,* August 16, 1963.

raphy, according to Johnson. A restrictive climate was forced on Palomar College by the verdict, contrary to the attitude of the students, faculty, and administration. The community had voted. The gap between the college and the community widened. A smear in print had become a valid, court-backed ruling.

Chapter 3

THE UNDERGROUND

> *Whatever authority*
> *I may have rests solely*
> *on knowing how little*
> *I know.*
>
> —SOCRATES

One of the first things a new group tries to do is tell its story. When existing media either will not or do not allow freedom of expression, a new publication is usually started to fill the void. Both *Playboy* and *The Village Voice* now represent established voices, and others have been started to give expression to dissident elements in our society. *Mad* magazine is another example of a way-out publication that now finds itself closer to the center of expression than when it was founded as a daring, extreme type of printed slap to the Establishment.

Underground newspapers associated with the hippie movement have even formed their own Underground Press Syndicate, through which member newspapers exchange articles. It claims two dozen members with a combined circulation of 264,000. The *Los Angeles Free Press* has a circulation of nearly 50,000 and covers riots and marches as well as the psychedelic scene.

Secondary schools may start an underground syndicate if the publications keep growing. Even junior high schools are now participating in what was once only for the daring in college. The colleges have been winning the battle to print what they want in the campus publication, but students at several universities, including Syracuse, have started off-campus papers to escape administrative censure.

27

The nonschool underground press is much more than a voice for the hippies. *Newsweek* interviewed several hippie editors:

The *San Francisco Oracle,* leader of the psychedelic wing of the UPS, ignores exposés in favor of ecstasies. "The *Oracle,*" says 27-year-old editor Allen Cohen, whose long, black locks are tied in a ponytail, "is more on the moon than it is underground." Graphically, the *Oracle* is illustrated with graceful and intricate full-color drawings. But the prose is often unreadable, drawing its inspiration from astrology, sacred texts of India, and the unedited musings of such popular gurus as Timothy Leary and Allen Ginsberg. "It's an oracle very much like the Delphic oracle," says one staff writer. "But there are no priests to interpret the babble. And so we just publish the babble."

Where do the undergrounders go from here? "We're simply chronicling the progess of the atomic children," says *East Village Other* editor Bowart. "We're for the young and the eternally young—the people open to change." [1]

UNDERGROUND PANEL

This could be the future pattern and appeal of the secondary-school underground, since hippies are prevalent among the high-school set. The American Civil Liberties Union has sponsored a panel discussion among editors of five high-school underground newspapers and members of the professional press:

By *Mary Reinholz*

The editors of five high-school underground newspapers met the press during a June 21 panel discussion sponsored by ACLU's newly formed Westside chapter.

The exchange between the fledgling journalists and three professional newsmen prompted a member of the audience to comment hotly, "This illustrates the generation gap—no, a ten-generation gap."

The conflict of generations, panelists, and audience began around 9 p.m. in Santa Monica's Madison school auditorium after the student editors had concluded a presentation on the origins of off-campus publications.

They complained of censored and trivial official high-school papers

[1] *Newsweek,* "Underground Trips," May 1, 1967.

UNDERGROUND PANEL—Four members of a Los Angeles panel on underground newspapers compare notes. Professional newsmen met with high-school underground editors in unusual public confrontation.

("90 percent on sports"), paternalistic administrative practices, and the "abridgment" of constitutional rights.

Some of their remarks constituted a criticism of the quality of education.

"Children are starving in Appalachia. Why aren't we learning about it?" asked Tony Andalman, editor of the off-campus *Worrier* and a student at University High School.

Cris Lundberg, editor of the underground *Sir Press* at Venice High School, said the school system taught democracy but didn't permit "students to practice it."

Both Lundberg and Geoff Birren, of Pacific Palisades High School, listed administrative strictures on hair and dress as examples.

Birren, editor of *Riptide,* said certain administrators questioned "the masculinity" of students who wore long hair.

Lundberg said the school security officer had visited his home after the first issue of *Sir Press* had been circulated. The security officer asked him if he were a "subversive Communist," Lundberg told an audience of about 50 persons.

When the editors (including Barry Tavlin of Hamilton High and Ira Schwartz of Santa Monica High) had finished speaking, KNBC newsman Bill Brown inquired:

"After all the ringing rhetoric, what is your basic complaint?"

Andalman replied, "Five administrators at University High School are controlling 3,500 students."

Brown repeated his question. Tavlin, an honor student and outgoing editor of *Insight* (the "oldest" paper in the high-school underground), said the complaint was basically a quest "for a decent education."

The off-campus papers, declared Tavlin, who will be attending Reed College in Oregon this fall, permit students to "quench their curiosity for learning."

CBS newsman Saul Halpert, deliberately critical, asked the student editors if they were "interested in dialog" and wondered how effectively they could present their ideas to a less sympathetic audience such as "the Kiwanis Club or the Chamber of Commerce."

In discussing the "effectiveness" of the student underground, Halpert said he detected an "incoherence" in student leaders he had previously interviewed while on assignment.

He stressed the need for "discipline."

Tavlin answered Halpert's comments. "I've been in every organization in the school," he said.

"We've [editors] turned down no attempt to discuss this with the community. We've permitted ourselves to be interviewed by the *Los Angeles Times,* the *Herald-Examiner,* and *Newsweek.*

"Maybe we don't write as well as adults. But we're trying."

Halpert's and Brown's remarks prompted an unidentified member in the audience to discuss the "generation gap" and to assure the students they didn't need to defend themselves.

"You've told us very clearly what your complaint is," he told the editors. "And if they [the newsmen] don't understand, it's because they're not listening."

When he said the editors reminded the adult press of "its own failures," the audience burst into loud applause.

When he sat down, John Waugh of the *Christian Science Monitor* commented humorously, "You must remember that we were brought here to be obnoxious," a remark which was greeted with laughter by the audience.

Ira Schwartz, editor of *The Voltaire,* said he agreed with Halpert about a "dialog," and criticized the ACLU chapter of "censorship by omission" in not presenting another point of view on the panel.

(Lorraine Oceans, program director, had announced earlier, however, that the chapter had invited school administrators to attend. All, she said, had "politely" declined.)

Scott Kivel, suspended and then reinstated at University High School after making a graduation speech critical of the administration, also criticized the effectiveness of the underground press.

"I understand what you are trying to say," Kivel said. "But what has *The Worrier* done about student problems?"

Andalman inferred that *The Worrier* may have helped create the climate which gave rise to a student demonstration which supported Kivel, but added the paper was only a partial solution to student problems.

The students were quizzed on whether they practiced censorship. Lundberg said he accepted anything "which won't bring us a libel suit."

The meeting concluded with Marc Cooper, editor of Fairfax High School's off-campus *Vista,* commenting on the purpose and effectiveness of the underground.

Like some of the panelists, Cooper said the underground had prompted the official high-school papers to introduce more controversy.

The underground press, he continued, gives "a voice to the students. Anything which helps fight the repression of students is effective." [1]

The refusal of administrators to attend seems to indicate that an impasse may be in the making. One of the major influences cited by the five editors was that the campus newspapers were almost shamed into extending coverage into previously taboo areas after the appearance of an underground newspaper.

JUNIOR-HIGH PROBLEMS

One junior-high underground newspaper was even credited with constructively aiding the school principal to revise the student dress code:

By *Ken Reich*
Times Staff Writer

Appearance of an "underground" student newspaper at Robert E. Peary Junior High School in Gardena has served as a catalyst in the revision of the school's dress codes.

Shortly after the unofficial, off-campus paper named *Predator* appeared, the school principal, Miss Kathleen M. McGuire, called a special meeting of 120 students, school personnel, and parents to consider a simplified, slightly more liberal dress code.

Peary, with an enrollment of nearly 3,000 students, is the largest junior high school in the Los Angeles Unified School District. It is only the latest of many schools to encounter the underground newspaper fad.

The editors of *Predator* included two students elected student body officers this spring at the school. Shortly after the newspaper appeared they approached Miss McGuire on their own to discuss their grievances, which centered almost exclusively on the dress code.

The two-page mimeographed newspaper had specifically called for the school to grant permission to boys to wear white polo-shirts and to girls to wear culottes and moccasins.

[1] American Civil Liberties Union *Open Forum*, July 1967.

Miss McGuire, in an interview, said actually she had suggested a simplification of the dress codes when she became principal last September. She said the process of consultation with students and others had slowly been going forward when the paper appeared, and she said its appearance had demonstrated "a lack of information or misinformation."

The paper had criticized the administration for rejecting "most, if not all, of the suggestions" made by students on dress, and one eighth-grade girl wrote:

"The students at Peary should be able to wear what they please. If the faculty doesn't like the way we dress why don't they buy every student a uniform? Then they won't have to worry about clothing, they could go on and do what they are supposed to do—try to develop our thinking."

The principal said she had learned about the impending distribution of the underground paper a few days in advance.

"I didn't have to go searching for the editors," she recalled. "They came in the next day and we had a talk about the rules. . . . We discussed about how hopefully they'd go about the correct procedures in expressing themselves the next time."

Reaction of principals to the underground publications has sharply varied from one school to another. A few principals have threatened or taken disciplinary reprisals, while others have adopted Miss McGuire's approach of trying to establish contact with the protesters and reason with them.

Miss McGuire noted that the undergrounders have become so common in the school system that the reaction of her fellow administrators when she reported that one had appeared at Peary was: "Welcome to the club."

Dress codes have been at issue in most schools. The general procedure is for the administrators to try to have the students play a prominent part in formulating the codes while at the same time holding a veto power in reserve.

Peary, as other schools, has its own regular school newspaper—*PearyScope*—which appears about four times a year. It has generally been bland. But the same day the underground *Predator* was distributed, the regular paper ran for the first time this year a column of "opinion."

"What's wrong with such minor displays of affection as a boy hold-

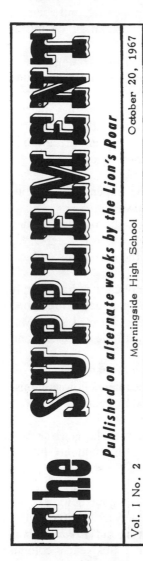

The SUPPLEMENT

Published on alternate weeks by the Lion's Roar

Vol. I No. 2   Morningside High School   October 20, 1967

New program

seeks to develop

competent drivers

"Driver Training is designed to make people m o r e knowledgeable dri- vers," said Mr. Jim Har- rick, driver training tea- cher, in an interview in which many of the ques- tions concerning the driver training course a t MHS were answered.

First, t h e course is for high school **students** b e t w e e n 15 1/2 and 18 years of age who wish to apply for a license. The course at MHS is open to

In our opinion...

Driver training endorsed

Of great interest to all MHS students of 15 1/2 or more years of age is the Driver Training Program. Driver Training must, by state law, have been successfully passed by any person between the ages of 15 1/2 and 18 applying for a learning permit. This law became ef- fective July 31 of this year.

The MHS Driver Training Program has been expand- ed to try to include all possible students. This has b e e n accomplished to an extent by providing driver training during PE classes. Of course, the 7th period PE classes, which contain the boys out for sports, can- not be curtailed for driver training purposes. Small numbers of these people will be able to take driver training on Saturdays. However, this part of the pro- gram is still in the planning stages.

anyone over 15 1/2 who has completed driver education with a passing grade. Students must sign up in their P.E. classes. However there has been some mix-up as to how boys with 7th period or 7:30 P.E. will enroll in the class.

Mr. Harrick commented that at the present time the present time the course gives preference to juniors and seniors, however, how ever, hopefully in the future the course will enroll all sophomores.

Presently there are 80 students enrolled in t h e course for a 28-day period. At the end of this period 80 more students will take the course and so on.

In the course itself, alternate days are spent in the simulator, a new unit at MHS which simulates actual driving, and actual driving under supervision. Altogether, a student spends 12 hours in the simulator, 3 hours actually driving, and 9 hours observing his fellow students drive. That leaves and extra 4 days in which make-ups and other details are completed.

We strongly endorse the new California statute and the prompt action taken by the MHS administration to increase the capabilities of the Driver Training Program. It is recognized that the law and the resultant behind-the wheel training for young drivers will make our highways much safer. It is hoped that other states will follow California's lead.

We seek contributors

In the first issue of The Supplement we mentioned that our pages will be open to all students and faculty members for the publication of letters-to-the-editor and well-written and researched articles of modest length.

We also mentioned that letters and articles may be of a critical or controversial nature (although personal attacks, frivolous opinionated material, or writings in questionable taste cannot be accepted).

This policy was established in response to numerous requests by students and faculty members.

As yet, we have not received any contributions from non-staff persons.

We hope that this does not indicate a lack of interest on the part of our readers.

We are honestly striving to provide a means of expression and a source of communication on this campus. There is definite need for greater communication between the students, faculty, and administration on this campus. Also, many people have a untapped writing ability and a need to express themselves.

We encourage our readers to respond to our offer and begin to contribute to our pages.

This is an unusual "underground" newspaper that is published by the regular school staff on alternate weeks.

ing a girl's hand on campus?" began the column by Richard Scaffidi, an eighth grader.

The regular paper invited students to submit "brief and rational reactions" to his views and promised to print them in the next paper.[1]

Why didn't the regular Peary newspaper editorialize on the dress code? Perhaps the editor and the adviser felt it was not the function of the school publication to campaign for student rights. Yet here was the perfect place to devote an entire page or issue to the question. Interviews with principals, teachers, students, and parents, including pictures of proper and improper dress, could have highlighted such a presentation. The alternative is the one-sided underground story that could easily contain errors in fact and be much more open to suit for libel.

A survey of nearly 200 high schools in southern California in the fall of 1967 revealed that seventeen underground newspapers were then being published. But even more significant, in fifty-two schools "rumblings" of planned papers were reported, and in twenty-one schools such papers had been published previously.

Many advisers cited the threat of an underground paper as a prod to both the regular newspaper and the administration to do a better job of reflecting true student opinion. Some principals met with staffs and encouraged freedom of expression, and one even held a noon-hour press conference to establish a dialogue with students.

The range of opinion expressed by advisers was extreme. Two felt that Communist groups were backing underground newspapers, others said that liberal parents were encouraging students to publish miniature editions of the adult underground press. One overworked teacher said she even had trouble putting out an above-ground newspaper.

One staff solved the problem, with administrative approval, by publishing its own "underground" edition on alternate weeks. Another school had the adviser of the regular newspaper also serve as adviser to the underground edition.

[1] *Los Angeles Times,* June 12, 1967.

An unusual situation occurred at one school when a militant volunteer teachers' association drew up a resolution backing the right of students to publish an underground newspaper. Although the resolution undoubtedly came from a small group, it does reflect the fact that certain teachers as well as students oppose the administrative "Establishment."

Here is the text of the resolution:

RESOLUTION
SUBMITTED BY THE POLITICAL ACTION COMMITTEE
OF THE LOCAL VTA CHAPTER FOR APPROVAL

WHEREAS, the VTA, which is the voluntary association of professional teachers representing the voice of the La Puente Union High School District, has as its major goal the teaching of children;

AND WHEREAS, in the teaching of children, the classroom teacher is in loco parentis;

AND WHEREAS, the teachers, while acting in the stead of the parents, have as their responsibility the monitoring of the curriculum content during that time that the children are entrusted in their charge (by state law—from the time the child leaves the home until he returns);

AND WHEREAS, in recent months a tiny minority of students has undertaken the penetration of the Workman High School Campus with an off-campus publication (*The Free Thinker*);

AND WHEREAS, these "underground" publications have caused considerable Faculty and Student division, we the VTA feel that a statement and stand is in order at this time.

The VTA position on off-campus publication is as follows:

1. We feel that the students are to be commended for having the curiosity to dwell upon social issues of the day.
2. We feel that they are to be commended even further for the follow-through they have shown in forming a newspaper, publishing it, and distributing it.
3. But we of the VTA, sensitive of our guardian status to the young entrusted to our charge, feel that this adolescent spirit of enquiry and concern needs to be encouraged into more positive channels:

   a. For one thing, we are justifiably concerned about the financing of such publication (for who does pay the piper? —and therefore call the tune).
   b. For another, we feel that for a publication to be regarded as "educationally worthy" it should be unbiased and impartial. We are concerned over the obvious bias and slant, and overenthusiastic preference for a political point of view which the recent *Free Thinkers* have manifested.
   c. And finally, when such uncontrolled publications actually advocate civil disobedience such as . . . "All boys sign a loyalty oath not to go back on the rest and march up the steps under the administration building and pull out their shirt tails. This will work—in unity there is strength." Such exuberance, we feel, should be educationally guided, lest negative learning should result.

We therefore suggest in a positive view, that we explore the possibility of enriching the content of our present student newspapers, perhaps encouraging the formation of a pro–con section of the student newspaper presenting the controversial issues of the day. To this, however, we append a strong caution, reminding all concerned that the student newspaper is a curriculum tool, and as such *must* abide by the educational code of presenting controversial issues fairly and without bias. There would need to be an *Impartial Editorial Committee* to supervise the balance of student editorial comments in these sections.

In conclusion, the VTA, again in the positive view of extending their friendly hand of professional brotherhood, would go on record as supporting our colleagues in the administration in any firm stand they may wish to take in their attempt to protect *our* La Puente youth against its own impulsive lack of experience.

Publicity is often an important factor in the publishing of an underground newspaper. Television or community newspaper exposure usually aids a group in getting funds and support to keep the off-campus publication going.

An article in a suburban California newspaper did an objective job of covering the debut of an underground newspaper at a nearby high school:

UNDERGROUND PAPER MAKES DEBUT AT RAMONA

Ramona High School's first "underground" newspaper had its debut on the campus yesterday taking a jab at the administration handling of the recent dual stabbing in the school parking lot.

Student reaction to the newspaper, the Ramona *Free Press,* appeared split. If anything, students seemed less than enthusiastic about the five-page mimeographed publication's first edition.

But the student editors were most amazed by the reaction of the Ramona administration.

"We've had a very fair response from the administration," said editor Dan Corcoran, a senior and member of the United Student Body at Ramona.

"It sort of shocked me," he said.

Actually, the newspaper is not an underground newspaper in the usual sense because it has the approval of the United Student Body, which is the official student government organization.

That approval means that the *Free Press* can be distributed on campus, unlike the publication called *It,* an underground newspaper published by a group of liberal activist students and banned from all Riverside Unified School District campuses.

The editors plan to make the *Free Press* a weekly publication and are charging 10 cents a copy. Sales were good yesterday, Corcoran said.

Although the first issue disputed some of the facts reported by the administration in the stabbing of George and Henry Lara two weeks ago, students seemed most riled by a column critical of Ramona cliques written by Ralph Gibson, vice president of the senior class.

The USB Cabinet yesterday, on a motion by Bob Hill, senior class president, ordered a rebuttal written in the *Free Press* disclaiming Gibson's charges of snobbishness among student government leaders, the Madrigals, the Lettermen and drama students.

But Corcoran is happy with that, saying that this kind of interchange is just what the newspaper hopes to accomplish.

"I'm not trying to cause trouble," he says. "I want to get a few people to use their brains."

"Ramona's a good school," he adds, "but it won't be a good school when people stop complaining."

Also unlike *It,* Ramona's new *Free Press*—at least in its first issue—sticks to high-school campus issues. Smoking on campus, selection of drama productions, and compulsory physical education are some of the other topics discussed.[1]

One adviser told of recruiting several students for her staff after an underground paper died in the thinking stage because of expense. Several advisers said that the only continuing underground newspapers are those subsidized by parents.

Perhaps the most humorous reply to the survey came from an editor of a high-school paper who said she published a story in her campus publication about underground newspapers in the hope of finding enough interest to start one. This naive young miss didn't mention the adviser, but said the regular paper was heavily censored.

Adviser Robert Ludwig of Edgewood High in West Covina summed up the feelings of many teachers in his reply:

"We no longer live in a time when all responsible citizens are consistently obedient and respectful to all wishes of authority organs. Ours is a restless age and our students question and react. As teachers and administrators we cannot be arbitrary; we cannot be insensitive; we must practice the values we teach. It is my opinion that too rigid censorship—an insensitivity to the needs of adolescents, has forced many papers underground.

"The right of a school district administration to define the type of newspaper they will allow is beyond question. The adviser's handbook published by the National Scholastic Press Association sets forth four entirely different types of high-school newspapers by the function they are created to perform. There is little uniformity of purpose between districts. Indeed, there is little uniformity within districts. Very few administrators are really sure what the paper is supposed to do; and thus students are vulnerable to arbitrary emotional reaction. It doesn't take much of this kind of thing to send a paper underground.

"I urge that a statement of recommendation to school boards and administrators be formulated as a result of this survey. It might go something like this: 'Because we live in a time when conditions are

[1] Riverside *Press-Enterprise,* Oct 12, 1967.

such and such, because the formation of underground newspapers seems to be caused by such and such, and because this and this are the types of unfavorable things that underground newspapers bring, we recommend the following as the proper role of a high-school newspaper in southern California.'

"Figures about the number of underground papers in the area are interesting, but they are valueless unless we use them to help all concerned better understand the problem and the reasons for the problem. We can't halt the changing pattern of our society, but we can try to keep more papers from being forced underground. Let's get the newspaper back in the classroom where the teacher can help guide our young people so that their expression is responsible, free from libel, and in good taste."

A sister at a small private school told of serving as adviser to an underground publication so that "instead of being the libelous little rag the first edition was, the paper became a literary magazine in which the students defied convention instead of authority. Frankly, I feel that underground papers are put out by the intelligent child who lacks challenge or is too lazy to accept the everyday challenge. Too many advisers are concerned with winning an N.S.P.A. award rather than letting the students publish a newspaper. Our girls elect journalism. They design, lay out, and write the annual and newspaper. That is, they do since I took over. I let them try what they want. If they are in error, what has been lost? I assure you, nothing is lost other than a small prop under my vanity."

The influence of the underground on the official school newspaper was the subject of a story in a community newspaper on the outskirts of Los Angeles.

Last fall and spring, students from at least three South Bay high schools were busily publishing underground newspapers.

Today the underground printing presses in the area appear silent, although rumblings indicate more off-campus publications may be forthcoming.

Thus far, South Bay experimentation in high-school under-grounding has been held to a minimum, and the off-campus operations—composed usually of a one- or two-page crudely mimeographed sheet—have folded after two or three issues were published.

Editors of official high-school newspapers feel the under-ground publications often present legitimate complaints. But more often they feel undergrounding is just a fad explaining its current moribund state.

Nevertheless, in each instance where an underground paper cropped up, there was a noticeable effect on the official campus newspaper.

"The underground newspaper here helped us quite a bit, be-cause it awakened us to the fact that the student body wanted to hear both sides," said Debbie Ohlman, one of two editors-in-chief of *Sword and Shield,* the official newspaper at Torrance's South High School.

The *7 o'clock News,* which like most underground newspapers was short-lived, was critical of the policy of *Sword and Shield* because it "felt we were a rubber stamp for the student council," said Hunt Miller, the other editor-in-chief.

Both editors agreed that the off-campus publication made the administration more receptive to the views of the student body.

"It was a combination of a number of things," said Miller. "The council was kind of apart, and the newspaper and the administration weren't sensitive enough to the heartbeat of the campus."

At Mira Costa High School in Manhattan Beach, junior Tim Purpus freely discussed his part last year in publishing *La Otra Vista* (The Other View), the off-campus counterpart of the school's official newspaper, *La Vista.*

"Actually, we did have something to say at first," said Purpus, who is chief editorial writer of *La Vista* this semester. "But then it got be a gripe sheet with no basis—things like 'food at the cafeteria is terrible, blah.' The administration ignored it and it pretty well exhausted itself."

But again, the very existence of such a newspaper makes student journalists aware of their editorial responsibilities.

"We decided to give the students something more this year," said Kendra Fleagle, editor of *La Vista*. "As a result the kids seem more interested. I really don't think the faculty was responsible (for necessitating *La Otra Vista*).

"I'm afraid we at the newspaper have to take the blame, because the editorial content the last few years has been quite a drag, pretty wishy-washy."

La Vista's editor and chief editorial writer, both of whom feel they "aren't that capable of intelligently discussing world affairs," restrict editorials to matters which directly or indirectly affect the campus, although Mira Costa students are encouraged to write "letters to the editor" on social, national, and international affairs.

The *North Wind,* the bi-monthly publication at Torrance's North High School, last May nipped the problem in the bud before the second edition of an underground newspaper could even be printed.

Dan Brooks, then editor-in-chief of *North Wind,* directed a front-page editorial at *The Mole,* an off-campus sheet which died after the first issue.

"Anyone with a little desire and a little intelligence can write an anonymous article for an anonymous pamphlet," Brooks wrote. "But it takes a person with courage to put his name on an article and submit it to the school newspaper where it would be subject to a rebuttal, printed with the complaint.

"Any article or idea which is sincere, responsible, and represents the thoughtful opinion of a student will be considered for publication."

The majority of South Bay high-school campuses have not been exposed to underground newspapers. But this isn't to say students at some of these schools feel an off-campus publication is unnecessary to express their views.

"I think the school newspaper is the better approach because it is less of a hassle, but we are being forced to go underground," said a Torrance West High School student. He feels opinion in the official school paper, *Smoke Signals,* is too heavily censored.

He said plans call for an off-campus newspaper which will consist "mostly of stories that the official paper won't print. We'll stick mostly to constructive criticism on school matters and things about teens.

"We have no intention of going into the four-letter word business, and we probably will not have more than a couple of issues. But we hope it will make the administration sit up and take notice and realize we have a point."

Cathy Focarazzo, co-editor of *Smoke Signals,* said she agrees that any remotely controversial topic is suppressed in the school paper.

"We have to be careful about criticizing school policy," she said. "We had no 'letters to the editor' until this year, but we will still be restricted. There should be some censorship, naturally, but it should be lifted somewhat because we can get more out of our staff if there's more freedom."

Asked about the possible publication of an underground newspaper, she said, "If it's constructive criticism and there for a purpose, I think it's warranted."

Talk of establishing an off-campus publication at Redondo Union High School never went beyond the talking stage.

"A group one time wanted to start one, because they felt the school paper wasn't publishing all it could," said Rachel Hickerson, editor of *High Tide,* which received the University of Southern California School of Journalism's Crombie Allen Award for excellence.

"We can't print anything controversial here. The favorite topic is, say, 'school spirit'. Actually, the paper is a product of what the school wants us to be."

Most editors in the South Bay, however, feel students at their

schools have carte blanche on newspaper opinions as long as
the bounds of good taste are not overstepped.

Thus, publication of an underground paper to expose their
beliefs and feelings is not a requisite.

Said Susie Buckingham, a feature writer for the Hawthorne
High School *Cougar*: "There's no need for an underground paper
here. Some say we're running one every week." [1]

Some advisers allow staff members to work on undergrounders,
but of the seventeen reported off-campus publications, only seven
had current staff members working on them. Others had former
students editing or contributing to the underground. Several
schools pressured students not to work on such publications;
one extreme principal even made threats of expulsion from
school. Others instructed faculty members to discourage the
ringleaders from putting one out. This seems to reflect the mood
of the administrator. At schools whose principals were more secure and enlightened, an attempt was made to have the dissident
students use the campus paper to express legitimate opinion.
But in many schools where the "No Controversy" sign was the
order of the day, students saw no alternative to the underground.
A major conclusion of the survey is that the threat of an underground paper forces wavering principals to grant more editorial
freedom and motivates staffs to do a better job. Many advisers
like to "keep the lid on" and do not welcome "agitators" on
their staffs. As you know, the same criticisms made of the campus
press are often leveled at the community papers—and even at
several of the undergrounds. An examination of nearly two dozen
off-campus publications revealed poor printing, amateur editing
and layout, and much plain uninformed griping. Several papers
were poor imitations of anti-war, pro-hippy underground publications. A few were infantile reflections of poor campus papers,
screaming for more school spirit, shorter lunch lines, and cleaner
campus. Several included poetry and creative writing that was
excellent. Two or three expressed legitimate gripes and con-

[1] South Bay *Daily Breeze,* Nov. 5, 1967.

structive criticism, charging that the administration would not allow them a hearing in the campus paper. Many principals literally killed underground papers with kindness, thus disarming the militant students.

One underground editor claims that the off-campus publications are based on two concepts: first, the movement toward nonconformity, serving as a sounding board for any individual who feels he has a grievance; and second, and most important, to protest injustice. Several editors of official campus newspapers, however, point out that few of the underground editors have ever tried to work through regular channels. The assumption is often made, without fact, that the official paper won't handle certain stories. Personal attacks and libelous statements have no place in any publication, and a libel suit against an underground newspaper would quickly reveal this. Just as Monday-morning quarterbacks are quick to criticize the coach but seldom volunteer to take over, underground editors are finding the transition from verbal attacks to printed product difficult. It is far easier to evaluate than to equal the majority of campus newspapers. A survey of regular campus publications reveals as great a range in quality as in the underground editions. The answer is to upgrade the official newspapers, not retire to the basement without first making an attempt to convince administrators and advisers that responsible criticism has a place in the school press.

The majority of the advisers feel that the underground threat is just a passing fancy, yet several feel that strong backing, particularly from parents, could provide a base for regular off-campus publications. The cost of printing, however, would probably wear down financial backers, and graduation thin the ranks of editors. The overwhelming majority of underground papers seem dependent on one or two students for survival, and there is no organization for training new leaders. The attitude displayed by the adviser and the principal could well decide the fate of the underground, just as much as the community attitude. The appeal of illicit publications is always enhanced by school officials who make martyrs of the ever-growing number of young rebels. The underground high school press may die out, but it will have done more to force principals and advisers to re-examine editorial policy than anything else in student journalism.

Chapter 4

CENSORSHIP

> *The peculiar evil of*
> *silencing the expression*
> *of an opinion is that it is*
> *robbing the human race.*
> —JOHN STUART MILL

Problems of censorship are old and complex ones. News media have been accused of helping to create riots by coverage of incidents that seem to erupt through exposure. Yet the professional press has resisted efforts to have outside censorship of crime and trial stories. The cause-and-effect theory seems to have caused the dilemma. Does not printing a story really change the event? Historically there has not been precensorship in the United States. Libel laws insure that a publication is responsible for what it prints, but the only news management has been the reportorial and editorial limits of the publisher and his staff.

One of the basic misapprehensions of student editors and advisers is that the power of the publisher resides with them. Legally the power is with the administration and the school board, although ethically the students and adviser should have the responsibility. The students often graduate before they realize this responsibility, and the turnover among advisers is such that they very often do not accept the responsibility. Similar to the football coach who is fired for losing, the adviser is often replaced because he either will not or cannot settle the censorship battle between students and the administration. The adviser is the man in the middle.

Professor of journalism E. G. Blinn put it this way:

The editors of college and high-school newspapers operate under a particularly heavy burden. They must edit newspapers under a legal load unusual to the practice of journalism. That is, scholastic and collegiate editors do not have the legal protection of the First Amendment to the Constitution. Legally, school administrators, *in loco parentis,* have complete control over the school newspaper. Legally, those administrators may censor as they see fit.

I feel strongly that student newspapers should be placed under the protection of the First Amendment. *In loco parentis,* in this case, is not only destructive of potentially excellent young journalists but is, indeed, symptomatic of a disease that threatens society in general. This disease does not have a name, but is easy to diagnose. Its initial symptom is the phrase, "They are not old enough for responsibility," its terminal manifestation the words, "I will decide what goes into the paper." [1]

Many minors believe that they are not liable for their actions. But in California the law specifically cites where they are liable. According to the California Civil Code, Section 41, "A minor is civilly liable for damages caused by his wrongful or negligent conduct, but is not liable in exemplary damages, unless at the time of the act he was capable of knowing it was wrongful." [2]

School administrators are concerned with preventing controversy from being publicized. Yet this leads to censorship under the guise that the story might be libelous. There is no simple solution. The "don't rock the boat" philosophy leads to a successful administrative career. Public opinion is probably on the side of the administrator. Yet students and advisers in scholastic journalism are concerned with publications as exercises in academic freedom as well as vehicles of public relations.

[1] E. G. Blinn, "The Idea of Freedom," *Quill and Scroll,* February-March, 1964.

[2] Joseph F. Triska, *The Juvenile Laws of California.* Los Angeles: Research Publishing Company, 1950.

Paul Swensson, director of The Newspaper Fund, summed it up in an address before teachers:

The most tender area of discipline is not in generalizations of student behavior. It comes straight into the English and the journalism class and it rests on the question of censorship of the student newspaper.

"Freedom has its difficulties." That's the first sentence of an editorial on censorship in the *Oshkosh Index*. An afternoon of discussion could start at this point. One point needs to be made. Many of you do magnificent jobs of disciplining minds so that verbs follow subjects, and objects follow verbs. Tenses, genders, singulars, and plurals find their appointed places. You do amazingly well in chopping away the undergrowth of adjectives and adverbs which weaken sentences and the expression of ideas.

This is a necessary but tedious form of discipline. Try something more exciting. Find out if the boat rocks. Get into the heart of the problem of censorship of words and ideas. Academic freedom and freedom of the press can be understood by student minds. They are not too young to learn that freedom is earned through responsibility. If we simply pass it along from one student generation to the next, we lose it. This is the discipline of self which I hold essential for all who love to write.

If they love words, if they have a passion for facts, if they possess an understanding of the audience, and if they have learned something about discipline, they are deep in the pursuit of truth.

What reward shall you have for all this? Editors, some teachers say, are often too busy to care; fortunately this situation does not prevail in many Wisconsin towns and cities.

Sister Maura, whom I quoted earlier, reminds us that a "famous group of men asked a memorable teacher, 'Having done all these things, what reward shall we have?' " She continues:

"Every teacher of English has a private list of his rewards. It is hardly ever money in the pocket. But sometimes a teacher of writing reads a student's paper, not as a teacher, but as a reader; sometimes he knows that the standards he is setting in a high-school journalism or English class will influence generations; sometimes he sees a student of his become (in the teacher's lifetime) a mature and accepted artist. But the ultimate reward of the good teacher is to know that a student of his has grown in patience and tolerance, in creative discipline, in understanding of himself and others. He may even, by some rare miracle, bring his students to wisdom." [1]

THE OTHER VIEW

An opposite view and perhaps an extreme one is presented by John H. Duke of Fresno State College when he says:

. . . control must rest with the adviser. . . . Someone has to be boss! Power is not something to be divided into small strips and handed around. Like the politician, the business corporate executive, or the school administrator, the adviser heads an organization. If the publications are ever to meet their deadlines and be distributed to students, someone must make decisions and see that they are carried out. The problem of organizing the staff and the makeup of its hierarchy begins formally with the decision—"WHO RUNS THE SHOW." Advisers encounter here sometimes a "dualistic" theory which frequently clouds the picture and causes some wide-eyed idealists to advocate turning the publications over to the students as a constructive way of teaching the principles of "freedom of the press." This concept, however, conflicts with the fact that control must rest with the adviser. Confusion in this area is sheer NONSENSE! Every organization has direction and management. Professional newspapers are not operated by editors and staffs—regardless of freedom in the Constitution. The "freedom" guaranteed by this document is the right to publish a paper. The control rests with the persons who put up the money and stand to make the profits and losses. . . . THE BOARD OF EDUCATION is the ultimate authority for the paper—and can start and stop publications under the power invested in it by the PEOPLE OF THE COMMUNITY . . . students do not own the school newspaper or yearbook. The student EDITOR is not the PUBLISHER. [2]

This does not answer the problem of how to resolve differences between the adviser and the principal. I remember when a principal interviewed me as a teacher of journalism and asked

[1] Paul Swensson, "A Professional Journalist Looks at High School Composition," an address before Journalism Section of Wisconsin Council of Teachers of English, Milwaukee, Wisconsin, May 9, 1964.
[2] John H. Duke, "Who Runs the Show????" *The Publications Adviser*. San Joaquin Valley Scholastic Press Association, Fresno, California, 1960.

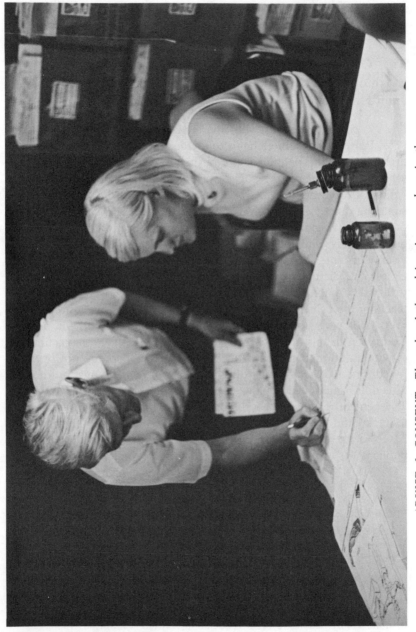

ADVISE & CONSENT—The role of the adviser is somewhere in the no-man's-land between student and administration. Photograph by Coates Crewe for Blair Summer School of Journalism.

what I would do if he told me not to print a story. I replied that I would look for another job if this happened too often. And by too often I meant more than once or twice unless there were extreme circumstances. The advisers and staff have to educate the administration and the student body as to what is a realistic and workable code for publishing the school newspaper. Obviously there must be restraints, but only to ensure good taste and avoid libel, not to silence unpopular opinions or opposition to policy.

A censorship case that concerned a magazine, although perhaps different from newspaper censorship, illustrates the student-teacher-administrator dilemma. The superintendents commenting on the case support the principal, although a recommendation for a review board is made in the dissenting opinion:

PROBLEM 121

Your high-school literary magazine has long been respected by both students and parents as a journal in which the brightest, most articulate students can freely express themselves. But the last issue includes one story, written by a 16-year-old honor student, that is liberally sprinkled with racial slurs and coarse language. It is a story about Southern families who teach their children to hate Negroes.

When the principal sees the story, he is shocked by what he feels is a breach of taste, and he orders all issues recalled.

The author and other students who staff the journal protest. "This is the language that the characters in the story use," says the editor. "Altering it would hurt the story."

The principal won't budge. "The story is going to be misinterpreted by many students and many people in the community," he says. "It will badly damage our image."

An English teacher, who is staff adviser to the journal, asks you to step in. "This is a beautiful, moral story," she says. "If we're going to discourage this kind of work by our students, maybe I should find a more enlightened place to work."

What action would you take?

CONSENSUS

Judging by the panel reaction, this is one of the toughest problems Administrators Forum has ever posed. One panel member quips: "If there is a sand bucket handy, I would be tempted to stick my head in it for a few days."

Despite the private anguish each panel member went through in reaching a decision, the consensus is clear: Back the principal.

"This situation is a perfect example of the age-old dilemma faced by school administrators, from junior high school through college," says Superintendent Daniel Taylor. "Stated simply, it is this: How do you give students an opportunity for meaningful self-expression without going beyond the bounds of good judgment and taste and reflecting unfavorably upon the entire district? If too little freedom is given students, the whole process becomes a sham; if too much freedom is given, severe criticism may be heaped upon the schools.

"In this particular situation, the principal, the staff adviser, the superintendent, and, at some later stage perhaps, the students, all must decide just what the purposes of the publication are. And they must establish procedures and guidelines that help realize these purposes. It's too late to apply this procedure now. The magazine has already been recalled. I would not overrule the principal and order it redistributed. I would, however, work toward getting all concerned to aim at a satisfactory procedure to be followed in the future.

"One possible future solution: Allow students to publish material that seems 'questionable.' But encourage the principal or some other staff member to write an accompanying statement that explains the position of the school.

"If, in the present instance, the English teacher is adamant in wanting the journal redistributed, then it may be indeed necessary for her to find a more enlightened place to work. If the principal has a long history of solid judgment and good thinking, I would certainly not reverse him on this one—even if it means losing a good teacher."

Our evaluator feels the principal is right in his decision. The principal, he says, must make his decisions in light of the total school picture, and he can do so without reflecting on the teacher's literary decisions.

"The English teacher speaks of finding a more 'enlightened' place to work," the evaluator says. "Possibly this has been one mistake that we all make today—our enlightened age has gotten out of hand. We need to revert back to some standards and regain our perspective. I agree with the action taken in this particular case, but I do somewhat disagree that we must always be so concerned with the school's image.

Many times our constant pursuit of 'images' prevents us from keeping abreast of changes in society. Fortunately or unfortunately, the teacher must work under present policies and directions of the school, and it is not for her to act contrary to them."

Seaford Superintendent Madden is in total agreement. "I would give wholehearted endorsement to the high-school principal," he says. "There will always be a gray area in decisions to curb freedom of expression. But this critical period of transition in race relations requires one to exercise, rather than to abdicate, responsibility for good judgment. Freedom of the press as an individual is considerably different from freedom as a member of a school group. The greater responsibility to a minority group overrides the freedom of an individual.

"When the public rebels and demands that heads roll, it is not the teachers or students who ride to the guillotine. If the teacher persists, after I have explained my point of view, then it would seem that she must be encouraged to seek employment elsewhere."

Praise the student for an excellent piece of literature. Commend the teacher for insisting that the creative writing mood of the student be respected. But then get to work on the problem of making the story suitable for public consumption.

That's the way another panelist would attack this problem.

"Racial slurs are important to communicate a realistic picture of existing and past discriminatory practices," he says. "Therefore, I would permit the use of racial slurs in the story. On the other hand, coarse language presents a different problem. To accept it from one student means to establish a policy that it will be accepted from all students. I would point out to the student, teacher, and parents that the writer's creative ability can be further tested by his ability to communicate coarse language without actually using it. I would then insist that this is the way it must be done. All issues would be recalled, pending a rewrite of the story."

Superintendent Norwood would table the article and ask the high-school principal to form a committee of students and staff members. The committee would develop a statement of standards for school publications. "Neither the superintendent nor the principal should cast himself in the role of censor," Norwood says. "The usual high-school staff and student body present a fairly good cross section of public opinion, and I am confident that a statement of standards would be reasonable and that the proposed article could be measured against these standards."

DISSENT

Chances are that the community may be more enlightened than the principal. The principal may be in danger of selling his school, and his community, short.

That's the way Larry Hughes looks at it.

"Suppression of the story will probably do more to 'damage our image'—whatever that means—than will its publication," Hughes says. "One of the risks you take when you encourage people to be creative is that they might rock the boat with their efforts. It's interesting to speculate about what people will think if the principal's initial decision holds. The assumption is made, of course, that what the student has written has real literary value and represents an honest expression of thought. If so, any bright, articulate student worth his salt would resign his position on the literary journal in disgust at the obvious inconsistency between what he is being encouraged to do . . . and what he will be permitted to do."

While Hughes thinks the principal erred in his judgment, he would not jump into the affray with fists flaying. He would talk to the principal, reason with him, argue with him, and *allow him to reverse his own decision*—rather than reverse it for him. "But it should be made clear," Hughes says, "that the superintendent must accept the prime responsibility in the event of any community uproar over the story. However, the possibility of any such uproar is slim in a community that takes pride in its literary publications."

But what about the future? How do you avoid a recurrence of this problem?

"This issue does present a Solomon-like dilemma," Hughes admits. "On the one hand, we have an individual proclaiming the value of the story; on the other hand, an individual proclaiming its vices. Is the superintendent to be faced with this kind of decision every time a breach in propriety by the literary journal is suggested? And what credentials does the superintendent hold to pass unerring judgment each time?

"This points up the need for some machinery to prevent this kind of trouble. A literary 'review board' might be one device to at least bring perspective to future problems. It's quite possible that the literary journal adviser *may not be omnipotent and unerring.* This literary board should be composed largely of teachers who can help reach decisions on questionable articles and stories. This board ought to be able to develop a general set of guidelines which would be of some help in questionable areas. These guidelines might also serve an instructional purpose. Extreme care should be taken, however, to prevent the board from becoming a censorship device. Ultimately this could evolve into a mechanism that would discourage the very creativity the magazine is attempting to foster." [1]

STUDENT REBELLION

Although the following case did not appear in the secondary-school press (since there were no more editions of the school newspaper), how would a school publication cover this type of story? The student-body president had to have his speeches approved in advance, which is censorship. Although the president was suspended because of criticism of the principal, the follow-up story in the *Los Angeles Times* hints that an armed truce was reached, probably because the president was graduating within a few days. This is the type of story that provides the basis for an underground newspaper (the school did have one), should the regular publication ignore it. The exposure in the *Times* almost forces the principal to allow the school newspaper to run some kind of story. Because of the time element, a news-feature treatment allowing both the president and the principal to present their views would seem realistic. The two stories:

By *Dorothy Townsend*
Times Staff Writer

University High School's 17-year-old student-body president was suspended Thursday after a surprise attack on the West Los Angeles School and its principal in his farewell speech at a student assembly.

About 2,000 students stayed out of afternoon classes for a time to protest the suspension.

After reviewing events of the school year as expected, Scott Kivel,

[1] *School Management,* November 1966.

a senior from Westwood, lashed out at the School's "deteriorating educational quality" and at Principal Hugh R. Foley.

Kivel said afterward he did not intend a personal attack on Foley but admitted using the principal's name and saying that "as long as he is here there will be strife."

Both Foley, 50, and Dr. Warren Steinberg, boys' vice principal, declined to comment Thursday, but a spokesman at the Board of Education confirmed that Kivel was suspended after the speech.

A suspension, the spokesman explained, is exclusion from classes and school activities pending the outcome of a conference with the student's parents.

Kivel's parents, Mr. and Mrs. Dan Kivel, 466 Dalehurst Ave., have an appointment to confer with Foley at 8:45 a.m. today.

Students heard about the suspension at lunch time, and a number of them stormed the principal's office asking questions. Foley did not come out to talk to them but Kivel did, one of the students said afterward.

"Scott told us the principal was not there and asked us to go back to class," said Tony Friedkin, 18, a classmate of Kivel's.

Friedkin said the attack came as a complete surprise to students and that its chief point seemed to be that the administration, particularly Foley, is "out of touch with the students."

"The only time I ever see him," said a miniskirted student, "is when he says 'Your skirt is too short; go to the office'."

"We are being treated like a bunch of kindergartners," complained a senior student.

"We could have had the Byrds (a rock-and-roll musical group) but he (Foley) wouldn't allow it."

Another complained that the principal is "never around—you never see him talking to anybody during lunch or recess."

The students dispersed to the school grounds, where Dr. Steinberg spoke to them, but they did not return immediately to class. By sixth period (last of the day), however, most of them were in their classrooms.

Kivel, a B-average student who has been accepted as a political science major at UC Berkeley next fall, said he had had "disagreements" with Foley previously but maintained his criticism was not "personal."

"He is a very nice man," Kivel said Thursday afternoon.

He said his speech was prepared in advance and that he had memorized it for presentation at three morning assemblies. He showed the first part of the speech to a faculty member for the customary approval, but did not include the last portion, which contained the critical remarks.

"I knew it would never be approved," he said.

After speaking at the first assembly, he said, he was asked by Dr. Steinberg to hand over the text of the talk to Dr. Sheila Bauer, girls' vice principal in charge of student activities.

"She took it to Foley's office," Kivel said.

At the two later assemblies Thursday morning, Kivel gave "abbreviated versions" of his talk, excluding some but not all of the criticisms, he said.

He had been scheduled to attend a Rotary luncheon with the principal and went to Foley's office on his own volition at the appointed time.

"He told me there was no alternative except to suspend me," Kivel recalled.

The student body of 3,000, which includes many students from exclusive West Side neighborhoods and a number of celebrities' youngsters, was abuzz through the afternoon.

Foley would not discuss the matter with the press but issued a statement through the Board of Education, defending the educational program at University High as "an excellent one."

"Communications are always open with any member of the student body or faculty," he said.

"I have an open-door policy. We believe a good relationship exists between the University High School administration and the majority of students on campus." [1]

By *Robert Rawitch*
Times Staff Writer

The student-body president of University High School, suspended for criticizing the quality of education at the school, has been reinstated with no additional punishment, it was announced Monday.

Scott Kivel, 17, will return to school today. He said no formal apology was asked for.

[1] *Los Angeles Times,* June 12, 1967.

"I stand by the statements that I made. And I have the evidence to prove the charges." Although he would not divulge the evidence, he said he was planning to pursue the problem through normal channels and "speak to administrators downtown."

Kivel's suspension last Thursday followed a speech he made in which he cited the "deteriorating educational quality in the school"— specifically naming the principal.

Principal Hugh R. Foley then suspended him under Rule 130 of the Board of Education Code, which states:

"No oral presentation shall include charges or complaints against any employee of the Board of Education."

"Scott is a young man who is idealistic and has had many ideas which we have jointly discussed. Some of these have been incorporated into the school," the principal said.

"School administrators must work within the framework of the established state law, school code, and Board of Education regulations. Often the requests for change made by young people are contrary to the provisions of these guidelines," he continued.

Foley took exception to Kivel's remarks of "educational deterioration" and pointed to the school's record on national advanced-placement examinations.

He said that out of the 60 students nationally who scored a five on the test (the highest score attainable), four came from University High.[1]

PUBLISHING PARADOX

Reporters on professional papers usually are censored by the publishers. These are crimes of omission more than commission. There is an acceptance of this view in professional journalism. As has been pointed out, the conflict develops when students feel that they, rather than the administration, have the publishing power. Ideally, students should be given both the freedom and the responsibility. But the public blames the administrator, not the student, for extreme or unpopular views. Just as the parent realizes that the child must eventually learn to walk by himself and will suffer several falls, the administrator must make the difficult decision to allow the student to express his opinions,

[1] *Los Angeles Times,* June 13, 1967.

fully aware that printed stumbles will follow. Both the adviser and the administrator should enforce minimum standards of good taste and encourage self-restraint. The humor of youth can lead to serious libel, as was evident in the Bickerton case. A definite line exists between the area of fair comment and criticism and that of defamation. This is why the students should have a knowledge of the laws of the press. The speed limit must be set, but freedom to maneuver within that limit should be encouraged.

This view of censorship is stressed in the statement made by authorities in Scarsdale when right-wingers attacked the books used by the schools in that New York community:

We do not minimize the dangers of Communistic and fascist indoctrination, but we want to meet these dangers in the American way. A state that fears to permit the expression of views alternative to those held by the majority is a state that does not trust itself. . . . Any sensible person would agree that there are risks involved in allowing young persons relatively free access to a wide range of reading material. Of course, there are risks. But we believe there are greater risks in any alternative procedure. Surely we have not, as a people, lost the courage to take the risks that are necessary for the preservation of freedom.

Earl Warren, Chief Justice of the Supreme Court, in a dissenting opinion on *Times Film Corp. v. Chicago,* 1961, commented on censorship as follows:

As early as 1644, John Milton, in an "Appeal for the Liberty of Unlicensed Printing," assailed an act of Parliament which had just been passed providing for censorship of the press previous to publication. He vigorously defended the right of every man to make public his honest views "without previous censure" and declared the impossibility of finding any man base enough to accept the office of censure and at the same time good enough to be allowed to perform its duties.[1]

[1] *U.S. Supreme Court Reports,* Vol. 5L. Ed. 2d.

The real test of liberty was summed up by Chief Justice Oliver Wendell Holmes in his classic statement:

If there is any principle of the Constitution that more imperatively calls for attachment than any other, it is the principle of free thought —not free thought for those who agree with us, but freedom for the thought we hate.[1]

Judge Leon Yankwich pointed out the heritage of freedom we have in this country when he wrote:

We should trust, as did the founders of our nation, the power of truth to overcome error, or what we consider heterodox doctrine. To use force to achieve this result is to snatch from truth its only means of victory. . . . In my view, it is not the majority who need protection against heterodox elements. But, rather, the explorative minorities need protection against official hysteria. . . . Some years ago, a great Southern editor, Julian Harris, uttered this warning to American editors: "If you remain silent today on vital matters and live questions, tomorrow when a crisis arises, you will not know how to speak. By your failure to use freedom you have slain it. And when freedom of speech dies, liberty of conscience will succumb." [2]

The moral and ethical responsibilities of publishing overlap the legal. Scholastic journalism is a curious paradox of practice being the actual game. Students develop journalism skills by writing for a school newspaper. Unlike other classroom tests, the newspaper is graded by the reading public, not by an instructor in a private atmosphere. The academic freedom of the classroom clashes with the inherent power of the publisher to control the views of his product.

The Rev. Theodore M. Hesburgh, S.C.S., president of the University of Notre Dame, gave the administrative view in a frank letter to his student body:

[1] *United States v. Schwimmer,* 1929, 279 U.S. 644.
[2] Leon R. Yankwich, *It's Libel or Contempt If You Print It.* Los Angeles: Parker & Company, 1950.

The Scholastic had moments of greatness and promise of being the best, rather than a mixture of the best and the worst ever. Several tendencies marred the greatness: An excessively negative attitude that felt called upon to scorn everything under God and to pontificate far beyond the limits of its writers' modest wisdom; bitter analysis that often missed the point by ignoring or misrepresenting the facts of the matter; rather crude and unkind personal criticisms; and on one occasion, an open lack of integrity on the part of those in charge that would have cost them their jobs anywhere else and here, too, if the university were indeed what they were depicting it to be. . . . The barricades were noisily manned for every cause of student freedom, be it good, bad or foolish . . . when the plug was finally pulled, the editors walked out and seemed to become martyrs, although I have always thought martyrdom required dying on the job, not giving up. . . . Neither do I consider faculty and students equal partners in the educative process here, since students by definition are here to study under the direction of the faculty, and to learn. Nor do I consider student leaders to be makers of broad university policy or wielders of pressure, except in their own domain.[1]

The blending of freedom and responsibility is one of the goals of scholastic journalism. The legal aspects are so intertwined that the total picture must be observed for a fair view of publications. Censorship should not be divorced from libel. The student should have the proper training to make the correct, mature decision himself. This self-discipline is the bridge between the independence of the student and the control of the administration. Unfortunately, many students do not receive adequate training; on the other hand, administrators are so quick to censor that the full implications of the problem are never in view. A student will always want to know why he cannot do something. When the reasons are fully explained and justified, the student should arrive at the correct decision himself.

Professor James H. Durbin, Jr., of the University of Southern California summed it up this way:

---

[1] "How Much Freedom for the Student Editor?" *The Quill*, September 1963.

Every hour of the day, over the length and breadth of the land, a chorus of amateur know-it-alls and impromptu censors lifts up its voice in a hymn of criticism, the refrain of which is so often that gorgeously inaccurate but always justifying line: "I'm only telling you this for your own good."

So there we are, at the heart of the matter. With our splendid insight we can see where the other person has gone wrong, or is likely to do so, and we find it only charitable to pass that perception on. The aim, we know so well, is entirely altruistic. Why stand by and watch people make mistakes, in action or judgment, if we can supply that vital bit of advice or warning? Ultimately, this correctional instinct is at the core of any act of censorship by which an individual is prevented from doing, saying, reading, or looking at whatever he wants to. In our opinion he may, if unchecked, either harm himself or possibly cause some injury or distress to others. Even though our democratic ideal is a situation in which necessary restraints are as few as possible, practical considerations often suggest that we should operate on a lower, or what is sometimes called a more "realistic" level where some kind of censorship must be imposed.[1]

The American concept of democracy is probably one of the major reasons for conflict between student and administrator. Durbin calls attention to the fact that there is a difference between what we teach and what we practice. The theoretical and the pragmatic approaches frustrate both the student and the administrator. The battle will continue because of an overabundance of courage by the students and an alarming lack of it by the administrators.

[1] James H. Durbin, "Literary Censorship," *University of Southern California Alumni Review,* December-January, 1963-64.

Chapter 5

FREEDOM: COLLEGE STYLE

> *Though all the winds of*
> *doctrine were let loose to play*
> *upon the earth, so Truth be in*
> *the field, we do ingloriously, by*
> *licensing and prohibiting, to*
> *misdoubt her strength. Let*
> *her and Falsehood grapple: who*
> *ever knew Truth put to the worse*
> *in a free and open encounter?*
> —JOHN MILTON

In secondary schools, where the question is whether the students should have freedom in college, the problem appears to be how much freedom they should have. Social critic Paul Goodman asserts that the past decade of unrest in higher education has been caused by the fight for the "right to learn" as opposed to the earlier "right to teach" struggle of professors. Thus, academic freedom now is being sought by the students instead of the instructors, and college newspapers have reflected this battle with the administration.

Ideally, journalism educators believe, the solution to the problem of editorial control is to "train 'em and trust 'em." The calculated risk of allowing editorial freedom can be dangerous when it backfires. Administrators can be divided into two camps, those who do believe in editorial freedom and those who do not. But even the latter group realize that in higher education students demand more expression and that prior restraint in publishing cannot always be enforced. More supervision and censorship usually are found where the administration is weakest and most insecure.

The best book on the subject is *Freedom and Censorship of the College Press* by Estrin and Sanderson. This compilation of articles would be most helpful to the secondary-school adviser in obtaining an overall view of the problem in higher education. An excellent dissertation on conflict and controversy was written by Ken Devol of San Fernando Valley (California) State College for his doctorate at the University of Southern California. The title is "Major Areas of Conflict in the Control of College and University Student Daily Newspapers in the United States."

Following are some varying views on editorial freedom as expressed by college administrators and instructors:

Edmund G. Williamson, dean of students at the University of Minnesota, wrote in 1963 that "to repress students' expression is indeed a subversion of the very mission of the educational institution."

In discussing the Notre Dame *Scholastic* suspension in 1963, *Commonweal* noted that "at no time did the criticism of the students threaten the real authority of the university." The magazine commented:

No one has ever devised a foolproof way of keeping free men from doing or saying irresponsible things; nor has anyone ever discovered a way of imposing a sense of responsibility on students.

Edward A. Fitzpatrick, president of Mount Mary College, Wisconsin, summarized in 1948 the feeling among a great many administrators:

So long as the publication is a student publication and keeps clearly within the institutional purpose, it would be wise to give students the opportunity to express themselves without censorship and to have students exercise control over the staff.

As Chancellor Harry Woodbury Chase of New York University pointed out in 1941, the ultimate test of freedom is the use one makes of it.

Mark Acuff, an officer of the United States Student Press Association and former editor of the New Mexico *Lobo,* cited another reason for a free and responsible student press:

That the United States commercial press has, by and large, abdicated its responsibilities in the realm of free expression and criticism is no reason why the student press should follow suit. In fact, it is an excellent reason why the student press must work all the harder to engender and encourage a campus dialogue—for the commercial press is run by accountants these days while the student press still is run by aspiring journalists.

It is traditionally within the pages of the student newspaper that the issues of the campus are debated—and sometimes resolved. The student press has a historic role on the campus as critic and gadfly, source of new ideas, and proposer of new solutions.

In urging maximum freedom for the campus press, Dwight Bentel of San Jose State College nonetheless summarized in 1956 one area of concern to those who argue for greater control.

The college editor is a transient. He comes . . . and goes.

During his four-year educational excursion across the campus from enrollment to graduation he pauses briefly to sample the duties of editorship, then moves along.

When he arrives the student newspaper is waiting for him, ready made. He had no part in its creation, has no financial stake in its success, is relatively unaffected by its continued well-being.

He brings to the editorship a limited experience, if any. His judgment is circumscribed by his years, his responsibility may or may not have outgrown his adolescence.

If his editorship causes embarrassment to the institution, administration, or faculty, or injury to the student body, or harm to the paper itself, at the end of his brief term he merely walks away from the wreckage.

Freedom of the press for the college editor, then, may be in large measure freedom without responsibility.

Hence, it is easy to sympathize with a college administration that clamps restraint on him.

President Irvin Stewart of West Virginia University said that he tended to deal directly with the student editors rather than with the advisers:

Where the facts do not appear to justify the criticism, we call that to the attention of the student editors. This is not with any view of seeking retractions but merely to see that errors are not perpetuated in succeeding issues.

President Stewart discussed in another article the student's right to disagree:

In my opinion the delegation to a student group of the authority to decide and to act carries with it the right to make mistakes; it implies the right to make decisions other than those which the university administration might have made in the same circumstances. Otherwise it is a mirage, a form without substance.

He was supported in this view by Robert Gordon Sproul, who in 1952, as president of the University of California, supported the student's right to dissent:

In spite of periodic exasperation, I believe it is good for a college or university to have a student body which is encouraged to think for itself by the existence of opportunity to make mistakes. After all, one of the basic freedoms we are all trying to protect is the freedom to criticize and complain—the freedom to "gripe."

He cited advantages to the student in this type of free student press and at the same time minimized the danger of damage to the university:

It is good for students to carry full responsibility for the policies and performance of a campus newspaper, and the mistakes they make are not only effective educationally, but are less important than the administration and public think at the time they occur.

Robert M. MacIver wrote in 1955 for the American Academic Freedom Project at Columbia University:

This, then, the freedom to express and to defend his views or his beliefs, the freedom to question and to differ, without authoritative repression and without scholastic penalization, is the academic freedom the student particularly needs.

At the present time it is particularly important that the campus should evoke and sustain this freedom. Outside the campus, the pressures making for conformism impinge strongly on him. Some of them are directed especially toward him.

Harold C. Hand of Stanford in 1938 noted that although 70 percent of the student editors thought they had complete freedom of discussion in their editorial columns, there was in reality no such freedom as long as the college president had the "power of expulsion." Hand added:

We take the position that democracy is seriously devitalized the moment any individual or group is successful in preventing the open and free discussion of conflicting ideologies. We also hold that college students can learn to discriminate between or among conflicting points of view, an ability which citizens in a democracy must possess if there is to be any democracy, only through actually dealing with controversial issues. We are convinced, further, that the college newspaper is failing to perform one of its most important functions when it fails to serve in this sense as a training ground for democracy.

To which Harold Taylor, former president of Sarah Lawrence College, said:

Without a spirit of trust in our colleges and faith in our young people, without a belief that we can settle our affairs with positive, bold, democratic action, we will move from one timid mistake to the next into ultimate failure.

The Rev. R. S. K. Seeley in *The Function of the University* described what is possibly an administrator's greatest fear from a free student press, then warned of what he termed a far greater danger:

Not infrequently there is danger of student activities drawing toward the University undesirable notoriety, either by some radical pronouncement or by offending the canons of good taste. Since the public mind is quick to attribute to an institution the behavior and attitude of some of its members, it may be claimed that unrestricted freedom may be detrimental to the total value of the University. In general, however, the danger is a small one. Public memory is short and the Universities can afford to set an example in showing an indifference to uninformed public opinion. There is far greater danger lest the University in its efforts to remain in good graces of influential friends may impose upon its students a standard of deadly mediocrity.

Further, one critic noted, "Banning does not ban ideas nor do expulsions expel them—rather . . . they have the contrary effect."

The American Civil Liberties Union, in stating that "the *public* interest is not served when the *academic* community is fearful of experimentation, controversy and dissent," has urged "full freedom of the press." And all students, it continued, "should take responsibility for helping to maintain a free academic community."

Roy French, retired director of the School of Journalism of the University of Southern California, approached the problem from the viewpoint of education for professional journalism:

　I feel sure that back of the printed phrase, "student owned and controlled campus newspaper," is an administration, an alumni group, or some sort of a corporation with legal standing. Obviously, a constantly shifting student editorial staff, ages 18 to 21, is not such a body.

What I would like to know is WHY it is a "moral obligation and a professional duty" to lie to students directly or by implication by telling them, teaching them, or even giving them "complete freedom

COLLEGE PROGRAMS—The publication problems in higher education usually receive more attention than in high schools and may include television. Photograph by Conrad Waldinger.

of the press" while they are in college since, obviously, they will never have it again during their entire life as journalists.

Oh, sure, they may become publishers and have it, almost, but that is because they are publishers. Not because they are journalists.

In the following case the adviser became the buffer between the students and the administration.

Suspension of the University of Redlands *Bulldog* in 1962 came at the hands of the student editors themselves, following an administrative decision to authorize the newspaper advisers to bar material from being published. Editors were joined in support of cancellation of the newspaper by members of the Student Council, the English Department faculty, and the faculty adviser. President George H. Armacost labeled the incident "much ado about nothing." Yet he did remove Stanley K. Freiberg, assistant professor of English, from his role as faculty adviser to the *Bulldog* for a "complete violation of confidence." Armacost said that he gave "no permission to make a public announcement of this."

Professor Freiberg issued the following statement in support of the students' action:

Initially, it must be noted that a college newspaper does not gain whatever freedom it enjoys due to the public heritage of the freedom of the press or the provisions of the First Amendment. Whatever freedom or independence a college newspaper possesses is conferred upon it by administrative respect for the tradition of free expression and the educational values derived therefrom. . . .

Any institution is capable of paying lip-service to freedom of expression and academic excellence; but it takes . . . a great deal of patience and forbearance to concede that a student critic—however wrong-headed he may be—should be permitted to express his opinions. . . .

Thus, one must be on guard against such statements as "It is assumed that the adviser will grant freedom to the editor and his staff in proportion to their ability to accept responsibility." Such a statement betrays a basic misunderstanding of the very nature of freedom. It assumes that freedom is some sort of commodity or medicine to be measured out in doses, rather than that freedom is an attitude of mind, an orientation toward life, a vital philosophy. . . .

When students come to feel (as members of the *Bulldog* staff evidently do) that there is more concern for the maintenance of a smooth-running administrative machine than for the safeguarding of the privilege to question, to air unpopular ideas, and to stretch the mind—bitterness, apathy, and disillusion are inevitable.

If students are to be educated, they must be encouraged to speak their minds. They will be troublesome, inarticulate, inaccurate, heretical; but a little embarrassment for the college is not too great a price for the development of the mind.

The National Council of College Publications Advisers has developed a "Code of Ethics," which includes the following:

[The adviser] should be a professional counselor whose chief responsibility is to give competent advice to student staff members in the areas to be served—editorial or business; a teacher whose responsibility is to explain and demonstrate; a critic who will pass judgment on the work done by the staff and who will commend excellence as well as point out fault; an adviser whom staff members will respect for professional ability and contribution to the college or university publications.

Must have personal and professional integrity and never condone the publication of falsehood in any form; be firm in opinions and conviction while reasonable toward the differing views of others; be sympathetic toward staff members, endeavoring to understand their viewpoints when they are divergent; seek to direct a staff toward editing a responsible publication that presents an unslanted report.

Should direct the staff or individual members whenever direction is needed but place as few restraints as possible upon them; never be a censor, but when staff members are intent on violating good taste, the laws of libel, or college or university principles, should be firm in pointing out such errors; make suggestions rather than give orders; be available for consultation at all times; instill in the staff a determination to make the publications as professional as possible by being truthful and recognizing that fidelity to the public interest is vital; lead the staff to recognize that the publication represents the college or university, and that the world beyond the campus will in part judge the college or university by the product, encourage accurate reporting and see that editorial opinions expressed are based on verified facts.[1]

Perhaps secondary-school advisers need a similar code. The colleges have demonstrated that the fight for freedom of the student press can be bloody and never-ending. Secondary-school advisers should be aware of the past battles in higher education in order to become aware of the importance of editorial freedom in their own situations.

[1] "Code of Ethics," adopted by the NCCPA, November 3, 1961.

Chapter 6

LEGAL RESTRICTIONS

> *But he that filches from me*
> *my good name*
> *Robs me of that which not*
> *enriches him,*
> *And makes me poor indeed.*
> —OTHELLO

The first line of defense against libel is the reporter. But unless he knows what libel is, the possibilities of error through ignorance are staggering. Teen-agers have to pass a test on driving regulations before they can get behind the wheel of a car, and young hunters are usually required to pass a safety test before shooting a deer; yet students sit down at a typewriter without the vaguest idea of the legal restrictions of journalism. As we have seen in the Bickerton yearbook case, a student's idea of humor can be very costly.

On professional newspapers, the majority of libel actions originate from inaccuracies of reporting, editing, or headline writing. In the student press, the few cases seem to indicate that the libelous material was left in because the students did not realize that it was libelous. Advisers themselves seem to know little about the legal limits of publishing. The Journalism Education Association is preparing a booklet on libel, but there are very few articles, much less books, to aid the new adviser. Even taking a Law of the Press course is not always too helpful in meeting the needs of student publishing. Paul Ashley's *Say It Safely* is a solid book for the beginner that is not too technical.

A short history of libel laws has been written by William Finley Swindler:

Libel has been variously defined. Blackstone, the classic English authority, wrote that it comprised any false statements about a person "which set him in an odious or ridiculous light, and thereby diminish his reputation." Chancellor James Kent, in his early nineteenth-century *Commentaries on American Law,* described libel as "a malicious publication, expressed either in printing or writing, or by signs or pictures, tending either to injure the memory of one dead, or the reputation of one alive, and expose him to public hatred, contempt, or ridicule. A malicious intent toward government, magistrates, or individuals, and an injurious or offensive tendency, must concur to constitute a libel." This is essentially a definition of criminal libel; and as this type of action declined in favor of civil suits, other definitions were attempted. Mr. Justice Clifford, of the Supreme Court of the United States, wrote in 1875:

Different definitions of slander are given by different commentators upon the subject; but it will be sufficient to say that oral slander, as a cause of action, may be divided into five classes, as follows: (1) Words falsely spoken of a person which impute to the party the commission of some criminal offense involving moral turpitude, for which the party, if the charge is true, may be indicted and punished. (2) Words falsely spoken of a person which impute that the party is infected with contagious disease, where, if the charge is true, it would exclude the party from society. (3) Defamatory words, falsely spoken of a person, which impute to the party unfitness to perform the duties of an office or employment of profit, or the want of integrity in the discharge of the duties of such an office or employment. (4) Defamatory words falsely spoken of a party which prejudice such party in his or her profession or trade. (5) Defamatory words falsely spoken of a person, which, though not in themselves actionable, occasion the party special damage. . . .

Certain words, all admit, are in themselves actionable, because the natural consequences of what they impute to the party is damage . . . but in all other cases the party who brings an action for words must show the damage he or she suffered by the false speaking of the other party (*Pollard v. Lyon,* 91 U.S. 225, 23 L. Ed. 308).

This statement had to do with slander, but it applies equally to libel; and courts in many jurisdictions have cited this definition as authority since it was handed down. Perhaps the most recent pronouncement is that of the American Law Institute in its *Restatement of the Law of Torts* (1938), which simply runs: "A communication is defamatory if it tends so to harm the reputation of another as to lower him in the estimation of the community or to deter third persons from associating or dealing with him."

The progressively more exact definition of libel, as a matter of historical fact, has been the practical means by which freedom of expression itself has been identified in Anglo-American law. In the English system of an unwritten constitution—or more precisely a constitution made up of the aggregate of public laws currently in force and interpreted in the sense given them by contemporary political conviction—this fundamental freedom has relied exclusively upon a progressive modification of the laws on defamation. The constitutional systems of most of the American states also reflect this historical or evolutionary development of press freedom through a curtailment of the common-law concepts of libel; typical of many state charters is the statement in the New York constitution:

> Every citizen may freely speak, write and publish his sentiments on all subjects, being responsible for the abuse of that right; and no law shall be passed to restrain or abridge the liberty of speech or of the press. In all criminal prosecutions or indictments for libels, the truth may be given in evidence to the jury; and if it shall appear to the jury that the matter charged as libelous is true, and was published with good motives and for justifiable ends, the party shall be acquitted; and the jury shall have the right to determine the law and the fact (Article I, Section 8).

"Every man has a right to a good name in his calling, be that calling never so mean," ran an ancient English case. The concept of personal reputation as something which could be protected in court, even though it is intangible, is one of the earliest propositions of English common law as well as of the Roman law which formed the basis of most Continental European jurisprudence. The church, in the age when ecclesiastical courts had independent authority to try cases, punished defamation as a sin. The law *De Scandalis Magnatum* was enacted to protect the reputations of great men of the realm who would not or could not institute legal action in defense of their good names when attacked by commoners. Because the state undertook this action as a means of enforcing respect and preserving the peace, defamation was conceived from the beginning to be a criminal as much as a civil cause. But civil actions, brought in the seignorial or manorial courts for injury to reputation, were frequent throughout the thirteenth and fourteenth centuries—the period in which English private law was crystallizing in the classic trilogy of contract, property, and tort—although the separate tort of defamation seems not to have become clearly identified until the sixteenth century. The general use of the printing press by the 1600's prompted the courts to distinguish between injury to reputation arising from oral defamation (later called slander) and the considerably wider effect of an injury arising from printed defamation or libel. In 1670, indeed, one English judge declared of an injurious publication that "although such words, spoken once without writing or publishing them would not be actionable, yet here, they being writ and published, which contains more malice than if they had been once spoken, they are actionable" (*King v. Lake,* Hardres, 470).

The struggle for freedom of the press from the seventeenth to the nineteenth centuries was essentially a struggle to limit the application of the criminal law of seditious libel. The trend away from criminal actions for libel, both in English and American courts, in the past eighty years has become so pronounced that such action, particularly against orthodox news media, is rare. Criminal libel in the form of sedition has disappeared entirely as a common-law offense.

The law of libel has manifestly undergone extensive refinement and change over the centuries. In the past fifty years much of this change has been the result of revised journalistic practices; in the nineteenth century the excesses of political party journalism, as well as the newswriting style which called for use of vigorous epithet and gratuitous comment intermingled with fact, brought many a newspaper to grief and litigation.

Changes in journalism have in some respects outstripped the law, which is notable (some would say notorious) for the slow process by which it develops new lines of reasoning. The broad distinction between libel and slander, made at a time when the printed word was incomparably more capable of circulating a damaging statement than was the spoken word, has obviously been rendered obsolete by the growth of radio; courts and legislatures alike have been hesitant to include the broadcast word within the definition of libel, or to restate or reinterpret the statutory provisions on slander which are almost universally inadequate to deal with the problem. The liability of individual newspapers for wire-service copy or syndicated materials over which they have no practical means of control or checking for accuracy, is still absolute under the long-recognized rule that everyone who repeats a libel is separately open to suit. . . .[1]

Libel can thus be defined as (1) a malicious published statement (2) which is false and (3) which holds up the person injured to public hatred, scorn, contempt, or ridicule, or (4) adversely affects him in his business or professional capacity. It may be either the subject of (5) a criminal action or (6) a civil action for damages.

Another interpretation of libel was made by E. Douglas Hamilton, an attorney, at the annual meeting of the Columbia Scholastic Press Advisers Association:

Let us first look at what constitutes a libelous publication. There are three elements.

First, there must be a publication. You may write as many dirty ditties as you wish in the privacy of your own room, but if you do not circulate them among others there is no publication and there is no libel. Indeed, even if you make an indecent proposal to the object of your communication and you permit no one but that person to see it, there has been no libel because the publication must reach a third party.

The second element is identification. The individual about whom the matter is written must be identified. He may, of course, be identified by name but he can also be identified in many other ways. Anything that will identify him to one reader will be sufficient.

---

[1] William Finley Swindler, *Problems of Law in Journalism*. New York: Macmillan Co., 1955.

Thirdly, the article must have the effect of injuring the victim in the eyes of a substantial number of the average people of the community.

For classification purposes, the injury can be committed in any of four ways.

First is an attack on a man's reputation, a charge of crime, fraud, dishonesty, immorality, or dishonorable conduct.

The second method of injuring one in the eyes of the community is to expose him to public ridicule and scorn, and thus deprive him of the right to enjoy normal social intercourse. Thus, it has been held libelous to compare a person to an animal whose habits and characteristics are revolting.

The Hearst papers some years ago—in an article on revolution—compared the leading wrestler of the day, when wrestling was a semi-honest sport, to a gorilla, and this was held libelous even though the similarities between Zbyszko and a gorilla were remarkable.

The third way of injuring one in the minds of a substantial number of the average people of the community is to charge that he is mentally defective or the victim of a loathsome and contagious disease. If you publicly charge that a man has a loathsome and contagious disease, it may interfere with his opportunity to make dates with beautiful girls, and so it is libelous.

Finally, there is the statement which prejudices one in his business or profession, such as a statement that a lawyer is a shyster, or that a doctor is a quack, or that a businessman is insolvent.

The best general definition of what constitutes a libel is this.

A newspaper publication is libelous if it identifies an individual to any reader and produces an ill opinion of the identified person in the eyes of a substantial number of the reasonable and intelligent people of the community. This, you will see, creates a standard rather than a group of fixed rules, and the standard is reached by balancing various conflicting interests—the interest of the individual in the protection of his reputation, the interest of the writer in expressing himself, and, finally, the interest of society in news and information. These interests are not constant; they vary from time to time, so what is defamatory depends somewhat on time and place.

Let me give you a few examples:

It would not, of course, be libelous today to say that a man left New York, went to Utah, and joined the Mormon Church. But there was very strong public feeling against the Mormons in the 19th century and it was held libelous in the 1880's to write just that.

It was not libelous in the 1930's to say that a man was a Communist, but public feeling against Communism has risen in recent years, and since the Second World War it has been held libelous to write that a man is a Communist.[1]

The most common libel action is the civil suit started by one inidvidual against another. In criminal libel, the state prosecutes an individual for inciting a riot or offending society; it is very rare. Defamation usually falls into two classifications, libel *per se* and *per quod*. It is usually libel *per se* to call someone a Communist or say a doctor is a quack. Attacking a female's reputation or moral character, as in the Bickerton case, is also libel *per se*. In libel *per quod,* the plaintiff must prove both that the statement was defamatory and that it caused him damage.

There are defenses against libel charges, but not many. Although the truth of a statement is a complete defense in most states, there are exceptions. Many times the defendant must also show that the statement was published with good motives and for justifiable ends. In the defense of truth, one has only to prove the substance or gist of the charge, not the literal accuracy. The burden of proof rests with the publisher. The concept of privilege that excludes judicial and legislative bodies from libel extends to newspapers to a qualified degree; the story must be fair, accurate, and without malice.

Another conditional defense is fair comment and criticism. This is usually limited to public figures, such as politicians, athletes, actors, coaches, etc. Those seeking public office, either elective or appointive, may be criticized on the basis of their fitness for the position. This is usually interpreted to mean that one may comment on the novel or the plays, either dramatic or athletic, but not upon the individual.

Although mitigating circumstances are not defenses, they can reduce the amount of damages. Mitigating circumstances usually

[1] E. Douglas Hamilton, "The Law of Libel and the School Press." *The Bulletin of the Columbia Scholastic Press Advisers Association,* March 1967.

are absence of malice and prompt retraction and correction. The types of damages a plaintiff may receive are general damages, special damages, and/or punitive damages. General damages are assumed and are awarded without proof of actual dollar loss; they vary with the nature of the injury or defamation and the proof of injury. Sometimes juries award nominal or 1-cent verdicts when there is no real damage, but only a technical violation. When the plaintiff can prove actual monetary loss, he may seek special damages. Lost wages or business revenue are usually cited. While general and special damages cover actual injury, punitive damages are intended to punish the libeler. This usually means that malice was involved.

The honest, although not correct, opinion of a writer about something that concerns the public is protected. In 1964 the U.S. Supreme Court ruled that even when facts as well as opinion are written of and concerning a public officer, so long as the defendant has published the matter without knowing it to be false or without reckless disregard as to its falsity, then there is a defense. This is known as the *New York Times* Rule. Prior to 1964 it was not recognized in all states.

Newsweek discussed the Court's decision extending the rule:

In a key ruling last week, the U.S. Supreme Court carefully extended the right of the press to report about people in public life without fear of libel. But at the same time, the Court offered a minimum set of standards it expects the press to follow in reporting and editing the news. The cases involved former Maj. Gen. Edwin A. Walker and University of Georgia athletic director Wallace Butts.

During the riots that followed James Meredith's admission to the University of Mississippi in October 1962, the Associated Press carried a story reporting that Walker had taken command of a crowd that charged Federal marshals. In March 1963 the *Saturday Evening Post* ran its widely publicized "The Story of a College Football Fix," accusing Butts of giving away his team's football strategy to University of Alabama coach Paul Bryant. Walker and Butts sued and won.

Considering the two cases together on appeal, the Court tossed out a $500,000 judgment for Walker against the AP but upheld the $460,000 judgment for Butts against the *Post*. In so doing the Court handed down its most important ruling on libel since its landmark *New York Times Co. vs. Sullivan* decision three years ago. At that time, the Court said a public official could not collect for libel unless he showed the publisher was guilty of "actual malice"—either printing a story known to be false or recklessly disregarding whether it was false or not.

In the Walker and Butts ruling the Court extended the protection of the Sullivan case to stories involving public figures as well. By the Court's definition both men were public figures, Walker because he threw himself into the "vortex of an important public controversy" and Butts by the very fact of his post.

On the test of actual malice the Court considered the reliability of the sources and the amount of time editors had to check the credibility of their accounts. In the Walker case, it ruled that the AP, which relied on the report of its own newsman, 21-year-old Van Savell, had acted responsibly. The AP, the Court said, "received the information from a correspondent . . . at the scene of the events and gave every indication of being trustworthy and competent. . . . Considering the necessity for rapid dissemination, nothing . . . gives the slightest hint of a severe departure from accepted publishing standards."

But in the Butts case, by a 5-to-4 decision, the Court ruled the *Post* behaved irresponsibly. *"The Saturday Evening Post,"* it said, "was anxious to change its image by instituting a policy of 'sophisticated muckraking,' and the pressure to produce a successful exposé might have induced a stretching of standards."

The Court noted that the *Post* knew that the source of its story, insurance salesman George Burnett, was on probation for passing bad checks. And, among other things, the Court said that *Post* editors did not look at Burnett's notes of a supposedly incriminating phone conversation between Butts and Bryant and did not screen films of the game to see if Burnett's information was accurate.

"The evidence showed that the Butts story was in no sense 'hot news' and the editors of the magazine recognized the need for a thorough investigation of the serious charges. Elementary precautions "were, nevertheless, ignored." [1]

[1] *Newsweek,* "Limits of Libel," June 26, 1967.

COLLEGE CASES

The problem with libel cases involving student publications is that they usually are settled out of court and are rarely even filed, because schools would rather avoid the publicity that trial brings. The college press, however, does have several cases that might guide the high-school journalist. Dr. Kenneth S. Devol of San Fernando Valley (Calif.) State College discussed several college libel trends and cases:

Clarence J. Bakken in his *Legal Basis for College Student Personnel Work* suggests that whether an individual institution is open to suit depends upon legislation of the state in which the college is located.

State-supported colleges, he wrote, generally are considered agencies of the state and as such are not open to suit unless the state legislature has so indicated. This concept was established in 1839 by the United States Supreme Court in *ex parte New York.*

Separate incorporation of the student publication may afford the college or university some protection, but institutions cannot be certain they will escape the necessity of answering a suit, according to Thomas E. Blackwell in *College Law.*

He warns of "the uncertainty as to the extent to which the court will respect the legal fiction of separate corporation identity in the event of suit, if the parent corporation continues to exercise any substantial degree of control over the subsidiary."

In a 1959 case, Vanderbilt University successfully defended its position as being separate from student publications.

The libel suit, *Langford vs. Vanderbilt University,* was filed against the university, the editor of the student newspaper, and the printer. The university, however, was dismissed from the suit upon providing evidence that 1) the newspaper was not a university publication, 2) there was no advance censorship, 3) no member of the staff was assigned as publications adviser, 4) students made their own contracts with printers, and 5) profits and losses belonged to the editor and business manager.

The case against the editor, however, was continued.

Miss Langford alleged that the newspaper had libeled her when it reported in its news pages the legal action she had brought against the college humor magazine.

Court records indicate that she had told the editor and reporter she wanted publicity in the case and directed the defendants to her lawyers, who informed them when the suits were filed.

In reporting the pleading in the humor magazine suit, the newspaper included the charges and pictures on which the humor magazine suit was based. The humor magazine had allegedly damaged the plaintiff by printing a picture of her as a child of two. Her father had delivered the picture to the printer of the magazine to be copied for a Christmas card.

In its decision, the court said there was no evidence of malice on the part of the newspaper editor and reporter, that the plaintiff had invited coverage, and that the defense of privilege was valid since the report in the newspaper was a fair and accurate report of papers filed in the court, even though no judicial action had been taken on them.

The verdict was directed for the defendants.

Also successful in 1965 was the defense of fair comment in a suit brought against the 1963–64 editor of the University of Arizona *Wildcat* and the head of the journalism department there. A student senator from the College of Law had charged that a *Wildcat* editorial criticizing him was false and defamatory. He had asked for $30,000.

The defense was based on the 1964 United States Supreme Court decision in *New York Times vs. Sullivan,* in which it was held generally that a public official cannot recover damages for a "defamatory falsehood" unless actual malice is proved. The defendants in the *Wildcat* editorial suit argued that the student newspaper was exercising fair comment of a public official within the university community. The court agreed.

Charges of libel against student journalists are not often heard in the courtroom, however. Usually, there are more expedient methods of disciplining "wayward" editors. The consensus of lawyers is that little can be usually gained by legal redress.

Also, principals involved in a potential libel action often would rather not be involved in the publicity that inevitably would accompany such a suit.

One significant exception, however, is a libel action still pending at this writing, more than a year after the alleged libel.

An assistant professor of English at California State College at Los Angeles filed a $200,000 libel suit against the executive editor of the student newspaper, the *College Times;* the Associated Students; "Ann Konrad," a pseudonym used by the writer of the alleged defamatory letter-to-the-editor; and 20 John Does. He has asked for $100,000 general damages and $100,000 exemplary damages.

The suit grew out of a controversy that has gained attention on campuses across the nation: the question of student evaluation of professors.

The plaintiff in this case had written an article which opposed the concept of such evaluation. It appeared in the *College Times* during Spring 1964.

During the summer session that followed, a letter highly critical of the professor appeared in the *Summer Times* over the name "Ann Konrad." The suit is based on the contents of that letter.

The significant questions of this case include: To what extent is a professor in a state institution considered a public employee, and as such, to what extent is he open to fair comment and criticism?

How extreme can such comment be before it ceases to be "fair"?

Is the *Summer Times* in which the letter appeared legally the same publication as the *College Times,* even though they publish under different names, at different times, at different frequencies, and to different audiences?

Did the professor's actions meet the demands of California's retraction statute, which requires specific steps for the plaintiff to follow if he is to obtain general damages?

Can the newspaper's published explanation of its actions in publishing the letter legally negate punitive damages or constitute a retraction? [1]

LIBEL PITFALLS

Dr. Dwight Bentel of the San Jose State Department of Journalism has published an excellent article concerning high-school libel. A former president of the American Society of Journalism School Administrators and *Editor and Publisher* staff member, Bentel has listed some of the pitfalls in scholastic journalism:

[1] Kenneth S. Devol, "Libel and the Student Press," *The Collegiate Journalist,* Winter, 1966.

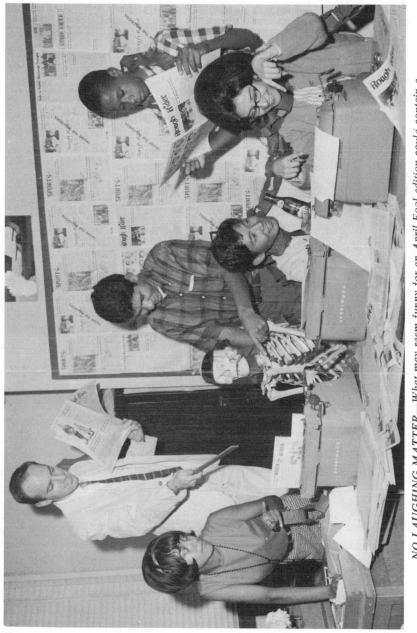

NO LAUGHING MATTER—What may seem funny for an April Fool edition could contain a libelous caption. The law has no humor. Photograph by Anthony Loya.

Even for the best-intentioned staffer, then, a review of some of the chief danger spots for student publications might not be amiss. Let's take a look:

LIBEL. In general, libel is printed defamation. Any charge or implication of illegal or immoral conduct, of unprofessional conduct, or of occupational incompetence may be libelous. It may be libelous to assert or imply that a person is mentally defective, or suffering from a loathsome and contagious disease. In short, any statement which injures a person's reputation or interferes with his right to normal social contact may be dangerous.

As I have observed the conduct of student publications over the years, it has seemed to me they are most likely to get into libel trouble over:

The gossip item. A juicy little boy-girl item may have disastrous legal implications. The law is very protective of a girl's reputation. Snide implications of questionable conduct or wrong-doing that so frequently find their way into gossip columns may backfire with stunning force. The gossip writer who thinks he is safe because he hasn't named names may wake up to find himself dead, because if any of the readers recognize who is being referred to, that does it.

The "razz" or April Fool edition. The law has no sense of humor. No matter how funny a defamatory article is intended to be, the law won't catch the joke. To headline the April Fool edition, in high glee, with a revelation that the student-body president has been arrested on a paternity complaint may split the sides of the readers— but it won't bring even a chuckle in the courtroom. A "humorous" item that placed boy and girl in dubious relationship may slay the reporter when he writes it—and later on too.

Student government. Defamatory statements made in courts of law or as part of legislative proceedings or official meetings are "privileged." That means if fairly and accurately reported by the press they are "safe." But a student court is not legally a court, no matter how judicial may appear the young dignitaries passing judgment on their wayward fellows. Student government is not legally recognized government, even though on its own school grounds it may govern like crazy. Hence, privilege does not apply to the coverage of what transpires in such bodies. A charge in student court that a club treasurer has misappropriated the organization's funds, for example, will be reported at the paper's own risk.

Criticism. Public acts of public officials may safely be criticized. (So far as the law is concerned. The student editor might well consider other uncomfortable possibilities before committing himself.) The paper may editorialize that the basketball team is badly coached, or the dean was arbitrary, unsympathetic, and unsocial in canceling the spring dance. But to say that the coach is incompetent, or the dean doesn't have all her marbles, is something else again. One may safely say (if he is fleet of foot) that the bulldog mascot of a rival school is "stupid." Animals cannot sue for libel.

Letters to the Editor. A publication is legally responsible for everything that appears in its columns . . . including the vituperation that may appear in a letter to the editor. Letter writers commonly tee off on objects of their wrath or scorn, then send their letters to the editor for publication instead of dropping them in the wastebasket where they belong. An editor's reluctance to publish such a letter may be countered with the statement, "But you're not saying it—I am. I'll take the responsibility."

Don't you believe it. The paper is legally responsible for everything it prints.

An idea is widely held that a newspaper may safely quote another's calumnies by simply attributing them to their source, or escape legal retaliation by saying "it is alleged." Not so. If your paper prints defamation, your paper, and those responsible for the paper, must take the rap.

Yearbook Captions. It sometimes happens that after a yearbook has identified the senior "most likely to succeed," "the biggest political wheel," "the warmest smile," "the most vivacious personality," it takes an uncomplimentary turn and discovers less commendable qualities among its constituency. At best this is a cruel practice. It also can be dangerous legally. So can captions under pictures in the life section that take a defamatory twist for the sake of "humor" or informality.[1]

---

[1] Dwight Bentel, "Has Your Paper Ever Been Sued?" *Student and Publisher,* March-April 1963.

One of the areas Bentel fails to mention is discipline reports. A student may be suspended for stealing hubcaps from a car in the parking lot, but the school newspaper publishes this at its own peril. This is not privileged material, since the police were not called in to press charges. Even if the police do press charges, there is the question of printing juvenile names. This is a matter for the administration and the staff to decide. Many professional papers do not print the names of persons under 18 years of age unless a major crime has been committed. Contrary to prevailing opinion, in most states this is a matter of ethics and not law.

The entire area of vandalism can be a difficult one. There is increasing pressure on professional papers to print the names of juveniles arrested for school vandalism. Some administrators feel that names of students suspended for fighting should be published in the school paper to serve as a deterrent. The Golden Rule, "Do unto others as you would have others do unto you," may be taking on a new interpretation.

Dr. Devol suggests other guidelines that can be established to help prevent libel suits:

Coverage of controversial issues, especially those involving courts, must be handled carefully.

Stories dealing with legal issues should be based on evidence submitted for the record, not on off-the-record hearsay, rumor, or statements. They should include the exact words and phrases used in the legal document, not a reporter's "augmented" version.

The newspaper must be prepared to prove the truth of the statements in question or to substantiate its right of fair comment or privilege. Repeating statements of others does not legally excuse the newspaper from answering to charges of libel.

Improper identification of persons can be disastrous. Simply deleting a name is not a dependable safeguard if the person is still identifiable—such as through his occupation or title, or if the person is likely to be confused with others.

Also disastrous can be journalistic attempts at humor, sarcasm, slang, and fictionalizing.

All letters to the editor should carry signatures and should contain such further identification as ID number, major, class, or address. Editors should contact writers if there is any question about the contents of the letters.

Headlines demand special care because of their attempts at brevity and impact.

Danger surrounds treatment of pictures in cropping, writing cutlines, juxtaposition, and makeup.

Corrections of serious errors should be straightforward. No attempt should be made to "weasel out" of the situation to fix blame, to be "cute" or to be argumentative.

When legal dangers are detected, editors should seek advice rather than to try to "doctor" the item or to disguise it.

If in doubt, kill it. An editor's hunch is often his best judgment.[1]

OTHER LIMITATIONS

Although libel is the major danger, the right of privacy and copyright should be mentioned. Lotteries are sometimes puzzlers also.

The recognition of the right of privacy stems from an article written in 1890 by Samuel Warren and Louis Brandeis in the *Harvard Law Review:*

The Press is overstepping in every direction the obvious bounds of propriety and decency. Gossip is no longer the resource of the idle and of the vicious, but has become a trade which is pursued with industry as well as effrontery. To satisfy a prurient taste the details of sexual relations are spread broadcast in the columns of the daily papers. To occupy the indolent column upon column is filled with idle gossip which can only be procured by intrusion upon the domestic circle.

Privacy, in legal circles, is generally regarded as being a purely personal right, which dies with the owner, and which is enforceable only by the individual publicized. Truth is not a defense for invasion of privacy, and the retraction statutes do not apply. Damages can be recovered for mental anguish alone, since malice

[1] Kenneth S. Devol, "Libel and the Student Press," *The Collegiate Journalist,* Winter, 1966.

and good faith are considered of no importance and special damages need not be proved. The major difference between invasion of privacy and libel is that the former concerns the effect of the publication on the standing of the plaintiff in the community. The standards used to judge privacy are those of the ordinary citizen, not the supersensitive. People involved in a news story may waive their right of privacy, but not always.

Two major rules should be followed by school publications:

(1) A person's name or photograph should not be used in an advertisement without his consent.

(2) A person's name or photograph should not be used without his consent in a fiction story or a fictionalized account of a past event unless there is a legitimate connection.

School publications must be wary of material submitted to them for publication. Student writers often plagiarize entire essays and features. There is the rare case of two persons producing similar works from a common source, which Judge Learned Hand summed up in setting forth the classic test of plagiarism:

. . . more must appear than mere similarity or even identity of the supposed infringement with the part in question. In this lies the one distinction between a patent and a copyright. One may infringe a patent by innocent reproduction of a machine patent but the law imposes no prohibition upon those, who, without copying, independently arrive at the precise combination of words or notes which have been copyrighted. (Morse v. Field, 127 F. Supp. 63; S.D. N.Y., 1954).

Copyright protects stories after they are written. When credit is given, a reasonable amount of copyrighted material may be quoted. Information is in the public domain, and facts cannot be copyrighted. The extent to which the author's style is duplicated is the key to plagiarism. Newspapers have the right to print the facts about a public happening, since these are available to all.

The danger in running news of lotteries is that U.S. postal laws forbid sending such news in the mail unless the item is clearly in the public interest. School clubs frequently seek to publicize raffles and door prizes. Some school publications are not mailed and thus are not affected by postal regulations. But advisers should be aware that lotteries are illegal in many states, and stories could result in loss of mailing privileges. The key to deciding whether or not an enterprise is a lottery is the requirement of skill. If the prize is awarded because someone has demonstrated skill with a rifle or throwing a baseball, it is not a lottery. The main ingredients of a lottery are prize, consideration, and chance.

Chapter 7

THE RIGHT TO REPORT

> To sin by silence when
> they should protest
> makes cowards of men.
>
> —ABRAHAM LINCOLN

Emmett Smith, journalism adviser of Cortez High School in Phoenix, Arizona, wants his students to have an experience and not just a class. He took the job of advising the *Campus Spectator* at the new school after an agreement with the administration that only quality students would be allowed on the staff. He felt that the best students make the news and only the best students should report the news. He also encouraged his students to interview prominent citizens in city, state, and national affairs. The late President John F. Kennedy, Barry M. Goldwater, Mrs. Dwight D. Eisenhower, John Birch Society founder Robert Welch, and various other personalities were interviewed.

The school board and a throwaway shopper newspaper took exception to a cartoon about Goldwater accompanying a story in the *Campus Spectator*. Arizona dailies and wire services picked up the story about the criticism of the journalism program. Smith fought for his policy of having students report off-campus news. He explained his philosophy in an article:

If we can't interview someone of importance in person, we'll get their views by mail. I want my students to know about the world in which they live. This equips them to become better professional writers.[1]

[1] Jerry Eaton, "We Cover the Nation at Cortez High School," *The Quill*, August 1967.

Goldwater, who lives in Phoenix, came to the rescue himself when it appeared that the student journalists would be restricted to reporting school news only. He defended the practice of permitting high-school writers to interview persons in public life and write interpretative stories about them. Thereafter the school board reversed its decision to prohibit students from conducting interviews with noneducators.

Thus we see that the freedom to publish news and comment is related to the corollary freedom to gather the news. The battle to report student-government meetings and campus elections is part of the war to gain access to public information on the professional front. Classified records, managed news, and Free Press vs. Fair Trial have made news in themselves recently. The last named especially has been the subject of several books and innumerable debates among bar, judge, and press. The essence of democratic government is that the people have a general right to examine the records maintained by their public servants. The entire concept of freedom of the press hinges on the ability to get these facts to report.

In an effort to ease the conflict between government and press, a Freedom of Information Act has been passed requiring Federal agencies to explain how they operate and to publish their orders, opinions, and policy statements. It requires that public records be made available upon request and permits a court test of government secrecy. The Department of Justice issued guidelines for the new law, and this excerpt from its preamble sums up the intent:

Free access to information fortifies public confidence and public understanding. It alleviates the dangers of government remote from human need. . . . Nothing dilutes the effectiveness of a democracy more than a government whose purposes, policies, and methods of operation are shrouded and impenetrable to the individual citizen.

THE PEOPLE'S RIGHT

The Free Press vs. Fair Trial debate was put into a larger and more relevant context by Carl E. Lindstrom by pointing out the

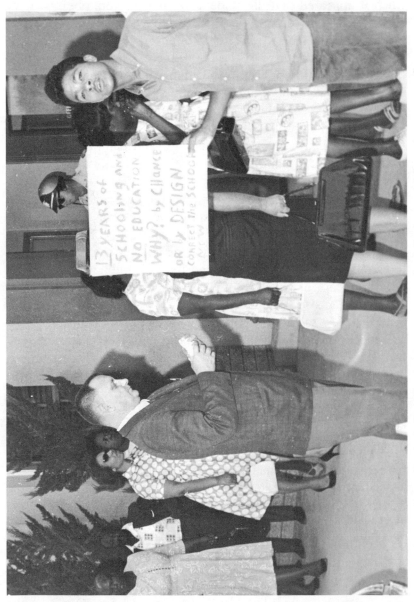

THE RIGHT TO KNOW—The decision to cover school-district news is one that many staffs have difficulty agreeing on. The militancy of the public often exceeds that of the students, and the professionals cover school events that the campus editors ignore. Photograph by San

failure of the press to be vigilant for the other three parts of the First Amendment. This is how the former editor and retired journalism professor regards the press and human rights:

In its own cause the press has not been silent, but it is my feeling that it will be faced with further erosion of its privileges in the future if it uses only the above-cited techniques which have so gallantly taken a licking in the past. What other techniques are there then, and what approaches? I cannot pretend to have a solution of our problem but I can point a route that has not been tried: *Get the people on our side.* They are not there now. The general public cares no more for a free press than it does for an old sock. Few people outside the profession know the importance of the guarantee, although, in the large, they are respecters of the Constitution. In its simplest terms: Let the press be as zealous in behalf of *all* human rights as it has been in defense of its own constitutional guarantee and I can see an enormous recruitment of public understanding. I do not mean civil rights, for in that department a majority, very close to the whole press, can pin medals on itself.

Editors are not likely to let the public forget that freedom of the press is guaranteed by the Constitution, but there is room for asking whether newspaper managements, editors, and writers are as sensitive as they ought to be about the other freedoms enclosed in the Bill of Rights.

Asked quickly to name them, some newspaper men might have to jog their memories. They feel perhaps that the church can with fervent jealousy look after religious liberty and that may be true. It is also true that the constitutional right to bear arms is obsolete as far as the citizenry is concerned and the privilege, except by license, is enjoyed only by those who live outside the law. But it is not true that freedom of speech is self-energizing and that the rights of assembly and petition can take care of themselves. Certainly the preconstitutional right of privacy, the eternal right to be let alone, needs guardians, first and foremost, strangely enough, from our hot hands as gentlemen of the press. . . .

Thus the most effective means for the press to preserve its own freedom is to be vigilant of the right of free speech, for if that is preserved and secured the others are in no danger. Let the rule work both ways: In a climate that permits unrestricted expression of thought the press needs no special guarantees. It could only restrict itself, a folly that would bring death on the vine because a right that is not exercised is bound to wither. The press has a custodial duty to watch over the right of free speech, which is the nerve ganglia, the soul, one might say, of the other rights. . . .

The press has control of the elements which might jeopardize a fair trial—publicity, the camera, editorial comment, the broadcast. The press resists the self-discipline of the bar, medicine, and the clergy. It is not sufficient to cling to a Coué-esque illusion that day by day in every way the press is getting better and better. If it cannot develop its own disciplines it should not be surprised if one day discipline is applied, the shadow of which has already fallen across its path. As a matter of fact, it is more than a shadow, for it is this that has already been applied by the high court.

If, in the Holmesian doctrine that the presence of the press at trials is to see to it that the courts are run right, who then is going to see to it that the press is run right? If an editor can justify his handling of a murder case that resulted in a mistrial and adds that under the same circumstances he would do it again, other editors can disagree with him but no organized journalistic body is set up to do so. Law, medicine, and the church have fixed boundaries for their areas of interest and can guard freedoms as well as punish trespass either from within or without. The press, it seems, must be so free as to be free from itself and its own regulation.

This dogma attracts strange companions—camels nosing around under the tent-flap of what they think constitutes a free press; pornographers looking for license, employers who once wanted exemption from labor laws, and more recently the right of History have been invoked. History has no rights, no absolutes—merely different versions of the unidentified flying objects that took like Truth.

Since the press has lost some important engagements, one can speculate that perhaps by galvanizing its interest in all the human rights it can attract public interest in and support for the right it treasures most.[1]

Two other problems are related to the right to gather the facts. One involves the presence of news media at the site of an

[1] Carl E. Lindstrom, "The Press and Human Rights," *The Quill,* July 1967.

event and their influence on the story; the other involves the right of a reporter to protect his sources.

Is television coverage itself a shaper of news? President Johnson has asked his Commission on Civil Disorders to determine what effects the mass media have on riots. This brings into the open the internal feud between newspapers and the electronic media. The 1967 riots in Detroit brought charges of inflammatory television coverage. Congressional and press leaders discussed the problem of riot coverage. Representative Durward G. Hall of Missouri told the House:

A sad but tragic fact is that our marvel of instant communications, with the potential to do so much good, mirrors the day-to-day events leading up to a riot in a fashion no less detestable than the worst days of yellow journalism.

National commentators on TV and radio decry what is happening today, but over many yesterdays they permitted their facilities to be used as incitement to riot and now they are reaping what they have sown.

A Stokely Carmichael calling for insurrection on a street-corner soapbox is a curiosity, a "hippie" talking to a few other "hippies."

But a Stokely Carmichael talking face to face to millions of people, recognized by those whose responsibility is to make sober judgment about whom to give mass media exposure, is immediately transformed from an oddball to a national figure.

Roger Tatarian, editor of United Press International, made this comment:

The question appears to be based on the premise that without the mass media there would have been no riots in Newark or Detroit or Milwaukee. To believe that is to display ignorance of the things that cause riots, and it would be a tragedy if at this late date the basic causes were not apparent to all.

In any event, the alternative to prompt and factual reporting by the media is to leave a vacuum for word of mouth and rumor to flourish. The incendiary effects of rumor in the climate that prevails in many places would be far more dangerous than the unadorned truth.

Among the comments received from broadcasters were the following:

William Sheehan, vice president and director of television news, American Broadcasting Company, said that television was willing to take its share of the blame for influencing news situations, but in many incidents TV "just is not involved."

He added, "We try to record the event, not shape it," and explained that ABC cameramen have instructions to cap the camera if their presence "starts changing the event."

Martin S. Hayden, editor of the *Detroit News,* said he believed television was "probably the biggest instigator of the riots here." He explained that he was not blaming TV, but said that it was in the nature of electronic journalism that such problems should arise. "People here watched those looters at work in Newark. They sat at home in front of their screens viewing the network coverage; then when the trouble started here many thought they'd get in on similar action."

Hayden admitted himself perplexed by the problem, saying, "I don't see how it can be controlled. It is a difficult area of responsibility to which electronic media must find the answers to new problems which are developing." [1]

In another decade, perhaps secondary schools will have educational-television channels covering student council meetings, elections, and extracurricular events. Would such coverage influence the news? The student journalist of tomorrow may have to find an answer.

THE BUCHANAN CASE

When Annette Buchanan, managing editor of the University of Oregon *Daily Emerald,* was found guilty of contempt of court in 1966 for refusing to divulge her news sources, national publicity resulted. The 20-year-old coed was fined $300 and sen-

---

[1] Tony Brenna, "Editors Give Views on Riot Coverage," *Editor & Publisher,* August 5, 1967.

tenced to a maximum of six months in prison. The case was appealed, but the conflict between the law and journalistic ethics began to be debated. Oregon does not have a "shield" law, as do several other states, to protect the right of the reporter not to reveal his news sources. Miss Buchanan, who gained her first taste of controversy by writing a stinging editorial at Ingraham (Wash.) High School, ran a story in the college newspaper on student use of marijuana. She interviewed seven students who had wanted to tell their side of the story. A district attorney subpoenaed the girl before the grand jury, but the editor refused to go back on her promise not to identify the students. The district attorney then filed suit and the judge found Miss Buchanan guilty. There was no question that the law backed the D.A., but sympathy for the girl was widespread. The D.A. was charged with harassing the girl for publicity purposes and failing to use his police power to conduct his own investigation.

This type of case could quite easily come up in the secondary-school press. And the underground press might pose another problem. How do such publications fit into the law? The student journalist who interviews LSD users and refuses to identify them could find himself in court, but unlike the Buchanan case, most district attorneys would probably not file suit.

Chapter 8

RESPONSIBILITY

> *Abuses of the freedom of speech*
> *ought to be repressed, but to*
> *whom dare we commit the power*
> *of doing it?*
> —BENJAMIN FRANKLIN

What do the mass media do?

The public functions of communication, according to Wilbur Schramm, are the same now as they were when the first tribes assembled on the beaches and in front of the caves. Schramm lists six functions of communication: it helps us watch the horizon, much like the ancient messenger bringing news; helps us correlate our response to the news on the horizon; helps us reach a consensus on social actions to be taken; helps us transmit the culture of our society to new members of that society; helps entertain us; and helps sell goods to keep our economy sound.

Four concepts of mass communication, also advanced by Schramm in *Responsibility in Mass Communication,* are authoritarianism, libertarianism, Soviet Communist authoritarianism, and social responsibility. When mass communication came into being around 1450, the society was authoritarian. Sovereigns and the Roman Catholic Church were great influences on the early press. A new theory of mass communication struggled to come alive during the 16th and 17th centuries. Libertarianism believed in private enterprise competing in an open market. Around the middle of the 19th century, a change began to take place with the advent of film. Then came Nazi Germany, Fascist Italy, and

Communist Russia with a new authoritarian theory. The mass media are the tool of the state. Meanwhile, the new theory of social responsibility began its turning away from the laissez-faire ethic. The press could no longer hide behind objectivity, but must also tell the truth about the fact. While libertarian freedom was negative, social responsibility is a positive freedom.

Are there comparable theories in the student press? The colleges have moved out of the authoritarian concept into a modified libertarianism that promises to grow into one closer to social responsibility. The secondary-school press is showing signs of breaking away from authoritarianism into a modified libertarianism. Can high-school students accept this type of responsibility? This question really probes into the entire educational system, not just the publications that are reflections of that system.

EDUCATION CRITICS

Let us look first at some of the critics. Dr. Edward Steinbrook, chairman of the department of psychiatry at the University of Southern California, told students:

. . . The "educational" systems of most modern societies operate on the false assumption, intentionally or unintentionally, that good character can be developed by telling stories of "virtuous" personages to children, by molding on the clay-like minds of the young that "God" will send to "Hell" those who commit sins: by developing a strong fear of God and the law of the land.

By the time one leaves college, he is coward enough not to break or question laws, to stay in the majority's fold and not to deviate from the average or normal norm of conduct—mediocrity, to be specific.

Most students leave school without: analytical perception—the ability to distinguish between assumptions, facts, between conclusions based on assumptions and facts: intellectual honesty—the ability to admit that many "truths" bandied about since time immemorial are nothing but useful "beautiful" lies, and to recognize them: and intellectual conviction—the courage, fortitude, and honesty to defend the truth.

The easiest kind of people to fool are fools, and these educational systems, by intent, carelessness, oversight, or plain stupidity, are very efficiently producing millions of fools every graduation year.

And when a person, organization, or state supports such educational institutions, it is clear as light that they had been, are and will always be up to nothing good.[1]

Nat Hentoff in *Playboy* defended "Youth—the Oppressed Majority" with his indictment of the educational system and almost a plea to move the authoritarianism to libertarianism. Some of his views:

In classes throughout the country, teachers ritualistically underline the importance of political commitment for citizens in a democracy. But the young are trained for this role in situations devoid of political activity. When a senior in a large suburban high school in New Jersey asked that the school's World Affairs Club be permitted to co-sponsor a lecture with an outside political organization, the director of student activities peremptorily informed him that no student political advocacy of any kind was permitted in the school. . . .

If the young are prohibited from learning how to govern themselves and from following their best instincts, including common sense, in high school, they do not receive appreciably more growing room in most colleges. There they continue to be prepared for the basic feeling of powerlessness of American life—the powerlessness of the individual, young or adult, to affect what Mayor Lindsay terms the "huge, authoritarian institutions that routinely cause fundamental dislocations in the lives of the people they affect each day." S. E. Luria, professor of biology at Massachusetts Institute of Technology, points out that "a most distressing aspect of university life is the mock parliamentarianism of formal campus democracy. Students engage in meaningless campaigns and elections for student governments that are concerned mainly with trivia such as curfew hours. . . . The empty, formal democracy of the campus is not only a frustrating experience; it becomes also a training ground for the acceptance of patterns of pseudodemocratic government, in which political machines

[1] Roger C. Birosel, "Illogical Campus Speakers Exemplify Results of Modern Educational System," *The Daily Trojan,* University of Southern California, 1966.

determine the choices presented to the voters, and a willful executive can frustrate the spirit of the Constitution by turning a legislative assembly into a rubber-stamp body."

Here, again, there is pathos in the repression of the young by adults. Those who are without power in the "real world"—without power in relation to the corporations that employ them, to the governments that make war and raise taxes in their name, to the social forces that make their cities unsafe and their air polluted—resent assumptions by the young that they can run *their* lives, that they can somehow avoid fundamental impotence. Father knows best, damn it. There is no hope. Settle down and hold onto a comfortable niche in the system. The son who defies authority shows up the weakness of his father and must be taught a lesson, the lesson being that passivity is wisdom, that survival is all.

The young, meanwhile, are prepared for "real life" not only by their subject status and by the meaningless regulations keeping them in place in the educational zoo. Also, what they are taught, as well as how they are taught, prepares them to fit smoothly into the system. One of the most basic of all needs—especially during adolescence—is to shape an identity, to find out what in the world is most relevant to you. But the American educational system operates all too often directly counter to that goal. The schools consider their function to be the adaptation of their pupils to the requirements of society as it is now and as they think it must develop. And increasingly, this is a society of specialization. Certain basic skills must be instilled to lay a foundation for the specialized skills to come. Recently, during the course of a series of lectures he delivered on the BBC, John Kenneth Galbraith asked: "Can we be altogether happy about education that is so motivated? There is the danger that it will be excessively vocational. We shall have a race of men who are strong on telemetry and space communications but who cannot read anything but a blueprint or write anything but a computer program."

But the schools, with few exceptions, have no time to worry about that question. Nor do they allow their pupils time to worry about who they are. Too much information has to be funneled into them so that they can go on to the "better" colleges and then to the "better" specialized jobs. The independent youngster with strong interests in particular areas that are not currently regarded as having a high degree of social usefulness gets in the way—particularly if he has questions for which answers are not to be found in the textbooks or the teachers at hand. He takes too much time and must either be cut to fit or leave school. He also gets in the way if his learning style is not geared to speedy achievement on predetermined tracks. . . .[1]

In another part of the article, Hentoff cited the case of Daniel Gladstone, a graduate of a large suburban high school in New Jersey. Gladstone told his story, "High School Students Have No Voice," in the *Saturday Review:*

During the past academic year college students dramatically redefined "academic freedom." What previously denoted freedom for professors to teach independently was invoked to mean freedom for students to advocate political issues and to participate in determining the courses universities and colleges offer.

That this redefined academic freedom is a reasonable demand on the part of students has been indicated by the success of demonstrations in its behalf. At Berkeley thousands of students came to Free Speech Movement rallies and, on one occasion, 800 were arrested. The demand has also received faculty support. Most conclusively, its soundness has been accepted officially at the University of California. There, starting last July first, "students . . . have the right of free expression and advocacy" although the University is able to regulate the time, place, and manner of such advocacy.

But what of high-school students? In comparison with college students they are obviously younger and consequently less mature; because usually only the top half of high-school graduates go on to college, they are, on the average, less intelligent; and because they have not studied politics and government as much, they are less knowledgeable in these fields. Nevertheless, both high-school and college students attend institutions of learning, some to learn skills needed upon graduation, some to prepare for further study. Though there are quantitative differences, there are qualitative similarities.

Despite these similarities, the freedom of political advocacy that college students have asked for and have to some extent received, does not exist in high schools.

Four years ago in my high school, a large suburban school, stu-

[1] Nat Hentoff, "Youth—the Oppressed Majority," *Playboy,* September 1967.

dents wore armbands during a Civil Defense drill to express their disapproval of such measures. They were told that they had to remove the armbands or face disciplinary action. A few months ago I asked the school's Director of Student Activities whether an outside political organization might cosponsor a lecture with the school's World Affairs Club. She told me that this absolutely could not be done, and she further explained that, in effect, no student political advocacy is permitted in the school. Students may wear political buttons only because they are "innocuous."

Yet many states have realized that contemporary political issues belong in the ken of high-school students and in the curriculum of high schools, and have instituted required courses in contemporary affairs including Communism. But student political advocacy could educate students vividly in these topics. If such advocacy existed along with impartial analysis of these courses, the influence of student agitators would not be excessive. Such freedom, instead, would provide politically motivated students with the opportunity to participate in activities related to these topics, and it would stimulate interest and opposition in other students.

As students in my school are not permitted to advocate political issues, they are not allowed to wield any actual power in governing their school or in appraising it. In the high schools with which I am acquainted only two organizations offer students the opportunity to act in these areas: the student council and the school newspaper.

Recently the student council of my school organized a committee to investigate an unsatisfactory cafeteria situation. The committee formulated several plans of varying complexity and expense for improving the lunch period. The administration rejected all the committee's suggestions and refused to talk to them beyond telling them not to bother with this problem, but to look into the trivial and probably insoluble matter of discarded silverware. The discouraged student council decided to ask permission of the administration to ask exactly what its powers were. Permission was granted, the question was asked, and the administration told the organization that the student council, a revocable privilege granted to students, is permitted to charter clubs, operate a lost-and-found, and survey situations with the consent of the administration.

I once wrote a review of a history textbook for my high-school newspaper. In it I established criteria for textbooks and showed how the book failed to meet them. Because the sponsor of the newspaper was not in school the day articles were sent to the printer, he did not see the review until it was published. Then, he, the vice-principal, and the chairman of the history department all told me that I had acted "out-of-line" in writing the review, and that I had no right to criticize an action of a faculty member or group.

When I spoke to the chairman of the history department, he told me that he agreed that the book was poor, and that replacements for it were being considered. When I asked him whether students might help select texts, he said no. But surely, if students had been able to help select the history text, this childish book would not have been chosen. Furthermore, if students were allowed to help choose all textbooks, and if they were allowed to help determine such matters as library selections, assembly programs, and student regulations, and if they were allowed to evaluate their education, the effect would be positive. They would be involved, and consequently more interested in their education. They would help choose teaching materials more interesting to them and help implement regulations fairer to them. It is an unfortunate irony that in a school that is designed solely for the student's benefit the student has no voice.[1]

Does a student have a right to criticize a textbook? Many students are not so mature and articulate as Gladstone, but surely the student press has a place for the "honors" journalist. Advisers complain about the poor quality of students, yet the top students will demand the right to write challenging stories.

ADMINISTRATIVE STANCE

An opposing view comes from conservative philosopher Russell Kirk. His traditional concepts interpret Gladstone's action as one of the excesses of the student editor today. Kirk's stance probably reflects the view of the administrator and the Establishment:

I hold that the student newspaper or magazine ought to enjoy a higher degree of freedom than does the public, commercial publica-

[1] Daniel Gladstone, "High School Students Have No Voice," *Saturday Review*, May 21, 1966.

tion; that is, the editors and contributors should be secure in a greater latitude of judgment and expression than are the editors and contributors to most periodicals. For the student press should share in the privileges and immunities of academic freedom. . . .

Now although academic freedom is primarily designed for the teachers and senior scholars in a university or college, it also extends in considerable degree to students. This was so in the medieval universities, and ought to be so still. Therefore it extends to the student press. The ordered liberty of the student press ought to be especially respected, indeed, because the press often claims to be the representative voice of the student body, and because it is a training-ground for responsible writing and publishing in the world beyond the Academy. Excesses of zeal, imprudence of judgment, and even intemperance of language ought often to be tolerated in the student press when similar offenses would not be tolerated in the ordinary press; for often it is better that the indiscretions and brashness of youthful judgment be endured than that the faculty of forming resolute opinions should be discouraged.

Let me suggest here, then, some of the more important rights and duties which pertain to the student press. Though I name the rights first, I emphasize that the duties are equally important.

First, the student press has the right to comment candidly and fairly upon the status of the students at the university or college in question, and upon educational problems and standards there.

Second, the student press has the right to discuss intelligently, so far as it is able, affairs beyond the bounds of the Academy.

Third, the student press has the right to publish the opinions and the original writing of such students as do work that deserves publication; and to print, so far as space allows, deserving writings from contributors outside the student body.

These are not the only rights of the student press; and these are not absolute liberties, but are subject to prudential considerations, as are all real rights; but this brief catalog may serve to suggest the nature of the privileges of the student press.

Now for the duties of the student press. If I name more duties than I name rights, it is not because I mean to burden student editors with obligations, but rather that student editors, like nearly everyone else nowadays, tend to talk much more about their rights than about their duties.

First, the student press has the duty of accuracy. The Academy being dedicated to Truth, and academic freedom being dependent upon respect for Truth, the student publications ought to be even more reliable than the general press.

Second, the student press has the duty of decency. Because it enjoys liberty, it ought not to indulge in license. The temptation to shock and scandalize ought to be resisted; the college paper ought not to imitate the gutter press. Ethical understanding is at least one of the principal ends of the higher learning, and college and university publications ought not to give the lie to the idea of a university.

Third, the student press has the duty of loyalty toward its sponsor or proprietor, the university or college. At most institutions, the college subsidizes student publications in some degree, and assures them continuity and protection. Commonly the college would be liable in suits at law for libel. The college makes possible the existence of such publications, in most cases. Therefore the student press ought to refrain from actions which would seriously discredit the parent institution, and possibly cause serious damage.

Fourth, the student press has the duty of respect for persons. It ought not to revile or ridicule college officers or faculty. While temperate and even severe criticism of the institution's policies and staff ought to be possible, this criticism should not degenerate into abuse, and it ought not to infringe upon the equally important academic freedom of professors. The student editor needs to bear in mind that the Academy is a physical and intellectual community and to exercise charity for the sake of the common interest.

This is no exhaustive list of the duties of the student press; but it may serve to suggest the nature of such obligations.

. . . The liberty of the student press does not include the license to foul one's own nest.

The rights of the student press, I am saying, ought to be broad; and the responsibilities of student editors ought to be serious. I am advocating the self-discipline which Dr. Kimpton commends among professors. The less control there is within, Burke observes, the more control there must be without. The real freedom of the student press is directly proportional to the decency and discretion, quite compatible with editorial vigor and independence, by which editors ought to govern themselves.

Students sometimes will do something just for the photographer in order to attract attention. This was obviously a posed shot. Photograph by Coates Crewe.

In conclusion, permit me to say a few words about the power of the student press. It can be considerable: not in the sense of influencing national elections or reproving the conduct of American foreign policy; but in the sense of developing real literary and editorial talents among the rising generation, and of forming students' opinion on the questions which most nearly concern them.

Some few student papers are so well financed and staffed, and connected with such large universities, that they can aspire to a format, a range, and a role very like that of successful commercial newspapers. Yet even these few—and certainly the great majority of student publications—ought to be concerned primarily not with covering the news round the globe, or with sermonizing on political and moral questions which puzzle the most accomplished statesmen and philosophers. The first concern of student publications, I hold—and the realm in which they can exercise the greatest influence for good—is the range of subjects and problems directly affecting the Academy. The improvement of academic standards; the struggle against apathy among students; the stimulating of students' discussion of philosophical, literary, scientific, and political questions; the encouragement of logical argument, lucid exposition, and spirited critical and creative writing—in such matters the student press can be superior to the popular press, and make itself worthy of the privileges of academic freedom. Mere clumsy imitation, with insufficient knowledge or experience, of commercial newspapers and magazines is unworthy of a college or university publication. Sometimes I hear it argued that a college paper ought to model itself on popular papers, and attempt coverage of scandal, politics, and professional sports, because the undergraduates can't be bothered to read an ordinary daily paper. Well, the Academy, after all, is a sanctuary; and there are advantages in being insulated, for a few years, from obsession with the giddy whirl of modern life. Modern man has been a good deal harmed by what D. H. Lawrence called "chewing the newspapers." If the student is to chew any newspaper, it ought to be a publication taking an intelligent interest in the life of the mind. A good student newspaper or magazine can do much to elevate, in the long run, what Arthur Machen called "that damnably vile business, journalism." [1]

[1] Russell Kirk, "The Freedom, Responsibility and Power of the Student Press," *The Responsibility of the Press,* Fleet Publishing Corporation, 1966.

PRESS FUNCTIONS

Does the student press fall under the heading of the "specialized" press? Dr. Walter Wilcox indicates that the college newspaper probably falls into this category. He writes:

The requirements of the press as set forth by The Commission on the Freedom of the Press:

(1) *A truthful, comprehensive, and intelligent account of the day's events in a context which gives it meaning.* This is a big order. The commercial press has a number of valuable aids which help it aspire to this goal, not the least of which are money, laws governing freedom of information, and the continuity which permits long-range planning. The college press is restricted, notably in the lack of privilege in source material and in the relatively inexperienced staffers upon which it relies. The college paper seldom has its community of coverage clearly assigned, and its responsibilities for coverage delimited.

(2) *A forum for the exchange of comment and criticism.* In this function, the college press could be expected to transcend the commercial press. Presumably the college is a fruitful source of ideas, opinion, and constructive thinking.

(3) *The presentation and clarification of the goals and values of society.* This is a rather vague and sometime function, and is probably used here in reference to the mass media collectively. This function when applied to the community rather than society as a whole is a legitimate one for the community newspaper. The college newspaper content must necessarily differ from the normal newspaper content because of the marked differences in "the goals and values" of the two communities.

(4) *The projection of a representative picture of the constituent groups in the society.* The college newspaper has a tough assignment here. It does not know precisely the various weights to assign its constituent groups because its function has never been clearly defined.

(5) *Full access to the day's intelligence.* Obviously, the members of a college community are not vested with the same "right" to intelligence concerning that community as are members of the normal

community, and this difference in the right to information reflects itself in the newspaper's function.

No systematic study of the function of the college newspaper in relation to its community has been done, at least to the knowledge of the writer. However, material concerned with manifestations of the problem proliferate. Usually, these manifestations occur following newspaper-administration conflicts, when educators, professionals, and even students make pronouncements. Occasionally, a thoughtful examination is essayed, but often these deal with manifestations of the function rather than the functions themselves.

Ernest Jerome Hopkins, professor of journalism at Arizona State College at Tempe, in a "swan song" backward look at his experience as a college newspaper adviser, has this to say:

"I found five distinct concepts as to the place and purpose of the college newspaper, none of which was that of a 'regular' or 'ordinary' newspaper on which a professional might work or train."

Hopkins lists these five concepts:

(1) The administration viewed the newspaper as an official publication whose utterances involved the entire college.

(2) The faculty viewed the newspaper as a medium of publicity, "departmental or personal, friendly or unfriendly . . . ; they were inclined to be jittery about it . . ."

(3) The student association viewed it as a house organ of the student government.

(4) The journalism students viewed it as their own.

(5) The journalism professor viewed it as a laboratory for training students.

None of these concepts was the entire story; all differentiated the campus paper from a normal community newspaper and put it into a class apart.

This was important, for each assumption carried its own inferences as to how the paper should be controlled. As a college house organ, it could and almost inevitably would be carefully censored. As a publicity medium, its editor would be a publicity man and its news values, pressagent values. As an Associated Students paper, it would be the political organ of the student politicians in office in any year, and if it criticized them, it might be sunk. As a staff-owned paper, it would be irresponsible, while as an academic laboratory it would be so over-responsible as to be unreadable. It was clear in my own mind that it wasn't my function to train house-organ editors, press agents, political apologists, campus sound-offs, or obedient nonentities . . .[1]

An ardent plea for change in the nation's newspapers was made by Alan Pritchard of the *Sacramento Bee.* The dilemma of the professional press pertains also to the student press. Yet many student journalists and advisers are unaware of this responsibility to meet the needs of the modern reader. Perhaps the realization that professional journalism is beset by some of the same problems may be comforting to the amateurs:

And in this sensitive, perilous, portentous situation, newspapers are in a nervous, uncertain posture, bent to outmoded goals, ignoring responsibilities, refusing criticism, laden with trivia and sensationalism. They are wracked with problems of their own: costs are up, as ever; automation comes but slowly; television is triumphant; morale is bad. Newspapers seek to move ahead by looking backwards and wonder why the best men desert to other fields and why readers zip through the headlines and turn on the television.

The reptilian eye in the parlor has irreversibly changed the pattern of life in these United States and has wrought a profound effect on newspapers generally. People have come to wind and set their lives by favorite television programs which, unfortunately for us all, are deliberately prepared to reach the lowest and broadest denominator of juvenile intelligence. . . .

Television does more than just take up the viewer's time. It mass-molds his intellect, changing his sense of values and setting his standards. And these values and standards include not only honky-tonk trash he accepts as drama and entertainment but what he accepts in the way of news. Surveys show that 55 percent (and some surveys go as high as 64 percent) of United States residents say they get most of their news from television.

"If that's the case," warned CBS newsman Walter Cronkite, who

---

[1] Dr. Walter Wilcox, "The College Newspaper—What Is Its Function?", *The College Press Review,* February 1958.

seems very aware of the dangers inherent in the situation, "then 55 percent of the public is inadequately informed.

"The problem is that we do such a good job, such a slick job in our presentation of the news that we have deluded the public into a belief that they are getting all they need to know from us."

Worse, Cronkite doesn't see that the newspapers are doing much to remedy the situation: "I think that you in the newspaper business are in some trouble because you are charged with a responsibility that you will not, or perhaps because of economic reasons you cannot, discharge. . . ."

Spot news coverage is no longer sufficient. What is needed is deeper digging at the underlying facts; clearer and more readable ways of writing; more enticing typographic presentation. How trippingly on the tongue rise these solutions. They should. They have been voiced a thousand times by convention speakers going hoarse with them. But the hearers heareth not. Or doeth not, which amounts to the same thing.

The basic function of the newspaper is to move information off the printed page and into the brain of the reader. Nothing should interfere with this function. No arbitrary rule of style should confuse it; no typographical flimflam should distract it; no dishonesty should weaken it. Everything must be calibrated to one principle: *Help the Reader Understand.* Any change that can accomplish this is already overdue.

There are so many things gasping for change. Something must be done, for example, about the dreadful sameness of radio and newspaper copy. Plug in the radio sometime and listen to a day's program. On some stations the news comes every few minutes—in bulletins, five-minute summaries, 15-minute roundups, and half-hour newscasts. By 5 p.m. you have heard the major stories of the day endlessly repeated. Pick up the evening paper and there are the self-same wire-service stories *in the self-same wire service words you have heard all day.* And listening, don't forget, is a tremendously less physical and intellectual effort than reading.

Newspaper writing itself needs to be changed. Stories can be written as stories with a beginning, a middle, and an end. The form they are now in was originated for Civil War telegraph transmission, with everything jammed into the first paragraph so that something that made sense would get through if the wires were cut. They don't cut wires much any more, but we do cut readership with this confusing story structure. We have conditioned the reader to be a scanner when he picks up his newspaper and sometimes I am not sure whether we even care that he doesn't read as long as he buys the product. We have got to change him back to a reader, and we can do it by writing events in the order they happened and in the form in which an observer might have seen them.

And if stories become stories, newspaper writers must become professionals with some liberty to be subjective, to feel and interpret as well as merely see and hear.

The advent of professionalism among newspapermen is long overdue. Not professionalism in the sense of being paid for practicing a singular technique as does a soldier or a Green Bay Packer, but professionalism in the sense of ethics and discipline and responsibility and freedom of decision akin to that in the fields of medicine, law, and engineering. Somehow we just never seem to reach any such destination.

Frankly, most of us are simply skilled technicians, craftsmen with words and pictures and presentation who work under orders for wages. Our major protest to slipshod publishing is the what-do-you-expect shrug and our typical comment is, "Don't look at me, I only work here."

Stories are assigned to us; we write them "objectively" from what we see and hear; our work is subject to editing by other faceless technicians versed in rotes of style and myths of nonsubjectivity. We are expected to take the X-ray but not to read the film—that analysis is reserved for the man who owns the equipment. Professionalism can't survive in such an environment; it can't even be conceived in it.

Lippmann in his London talk called professionalism "the most radical innovation since the press became free of government control and censorship. For it introduces into the conscience of the working journalist a commitment to seek the truth which is independent of and superior to all his other commitments—his commitment to publish newspapers that will sell, his commitment to his political party, his commitment even to promote the policies of his government."

Inevitably such a commitment to seek the truth will conflict with the interests and alliances of ownership. The pressure on publishers to occasionally ignore truth or stifle discussion can be enormous. And to a great extent it is the reaction to such pressures which determines the kind of paper that is published. Not every publisher may want the kind of newspaper that genuine professional standards would demand.

Whether we will ever reach a genuine professional status is much less important at this point than that we keep stretching for the goal. Like integration, professionalism is an emotional problem. To many publishers a full staff of professionals sounds like trouble but they may go along for a little tokenism. And working newsmen who are unqualified or fearful of the responsibilities of professionalism will always be with us; a whole commitment to truth can be a lonely and scary outpost.

The trouble with newspapers is not the many persons who run around wringing their hands saying, "The trouble with newspapers is . . ." The trouble with newspapers is that no one ever listens to the handwringers.

In 1904, Joseph Pulitzer wrote in the *North American Review:* "Nothing less than the highest ideals, the most scrupulous anxiety to do right, the most accurate knowledge of the problems it has to meet, and a sincere sense of moral responsibility will save journalism from a subservience to business interests, seeking selfish ends, antagonistic to public welfare."

Half a century ago Frank Moore Colby wrote: "Journalists have always been our most old-fashioned class, being too busy with the news of the day to lay aside the mental habits of 50 years before."

In its 1947 report the Commission on Freedom of the Press said that often today's journalist "means by news something that has happened within the last few hours which will attract the interest of the customers. The criteria of interest are recency or firstness, proximity, combat, human interest, and novelty. Such criteria limit accuracy and significance."

The late Max Aitken, Lord Beaverbrook, the Canadian-born press lord of England, said in 1964 at his 85th birthday anniversary: "I am not much impressed by all the talk about standards and codes. The code of a good journalist should be written on his heart. First, he must be true to himself. The man who is not true to himself is no journalist. He must show courage, independence, and initiative. He must be no respecter of persons but able to deal with the highest and the lowest on the same basis, which is regard for the public interest and determination to get at the facts."

And John Hay Whitney, publisher of the *New York Herald Trib-une*, on his acceptance of the 1964 honorary Elijah Lovejoy fellow-ship of Colby College, said: "We seem to have lost something: a spirit of independence, a spirit of our own ferocity, [and this loss] has made us captive to the press release and the gentlemanly code of going to great lengths to avoid embarrassing anyone.

"Our task is to cut through the junk in the public mind by seeking the order that underlies the clutter of small events; to winnow out of the apparent what is the real; to cede to television and radio the mere repetition of activities and to look behind the bare event for meanings.

"The role we can play every day, if we try, is to take the whole ex-perience of every day and shape it to involve the American man. It is our job to interest him in his community and to give his ideas the excitement they should have. These are the excellences of our craft."

Handwringers, all of them. But speaking from a deep understanding of the tremendously vital role newspapers play in our society. Too long have newspapers, the chroniclers of change, feared change vastly more than the senility which debilitates them. Too often have the handwringers been ignored; too often have we newsmen taken our responsibilities as journalists too lightly. For a nation confused by racial and sectional and idealistic differences may not be able to cope with a nuclear enemy. The sobering crux is that if our way of life perishes it will be because the newspapers failed first.[1]

Although you may feel that Pritchard is slightly overstating the case in the conclusion, the responsibility of student journal-ists and advisers could be even more strongly stated. High-school journalists who do nothing more than publish glorified "bulletin boards" are failing the educational systems as well as journalism. Advisers should take the leadership in meeting the responsibility that their positions demand.

[1] Alan Pritchard, "The Newspaper Responsibility," *The Quill,* August 1966.

Chapter 9

ALL THE NEWS THAT FITS, WE PRINT

> *Man's achievements rest upon*
> *the use of symbols.*
> —ALFRED KORZYBSKI

The great and gray *New York Times* boasts as its motto, "All the news that's fit to print." Student journalists, I would say jokingly, use a variation of this, "All the news that fits, we print." The point is that student publications, because of time and space limitations, are particularly vulnerable to indiscriminate trimming of stories. Real news management starts with the reporter, who sifts through his notes to select certain facts and quotes for his story. An elementary knowledge of semantics is useful for frustrated student reporters discovering the theory of non-allness the hard way. Too often the student does not study semantics until college, yet reporters should read a standard textbook, such as S. I. Hayakawa's *Language in Thought and Action,* before his senior year in publications.

One of the problems in the professional press is the growing tendency of reporters merely to rewrite the public-relations news release. Even in the editorial press, there have been startling disclosures, such as the fact that 82 newspapers used an editorial handout from a major company without changing a word or citing the source. The student journalist must be trained to attend the events that produce the news. This cannot be overemphasized. Too often reporters accept the statements of sources that have little relationship to the facts. The telephone and the postman are poor substitutes for being on the scene of the news.

There are limitations, of course, but the fundamental training should start with a reporter on the site.

Even this does not always insure an accurate account of the news. Student sports writers are often "one-eyed," seeing only the half of the field that is occupied by their team. One method of improving their writing is to compare stories with the paper of the other school and also the community daily. Reporters often accept statements from a person in authority without checking the information. *Time* magazine's interpretive writing has an authoritative ring to it, but the opinion that is scattered throughout the facts usually is considered objective rather than subjective writing. This type of deliberate manipulation is far different from that of the reporter who, without knowing it, passes along false information.

It is said that a reporter gets the story he is sent after and a good reporter gets the story he is not sent after. This is brought out in an article by Ken Macrorie. He tells of an incident that occurred in 1954 when he accompanied Peter Kihss of *The New York Times* on an assignment to cover a hearing of the Senate Internal Security Subcommittee of the Judiciary Committee. After the hearing, on Communist propaganda, Kihss discussed the story:

It had him stumped, he [Kihss] said, because the most important issue was not even taken up in the hearings. He had two alternatives, he thought: to write a short, straight story giving the facts, which were really old stuff except for the increased flow of material, or to write a long article in which he editorialized constantly in order to explain to the lay reader the significance of the whole controversy, and he would not be allowed to do that. . . . [After the story, Kihss and Macrorie sat down to discuss it.] I said that I [Macrorie] thought what a reporter decided to emphasize in a story made a great difference—no matter how fair or impartial he was trying to be. Mr. Kihss agreed, and as examples, typed off two possible "leads" for the story he had done. A reporter on one paper, he said, could understandably have written this lead:

United States' failure to recognize the menace of Communist propaganda was shown today when the Senate Internal Security Sub-committee brought out that Communist publications were entering the country on a vastly increased scale.

A reporter for another paper could have written this lead, he said:

The Senate Internal Security Subcommittee got into a competition for anti-Communist headlines with Senator Joe McCarthy's circuses today, when it staged a hearing on Communist propaganda—the first half hour being devoted entirely to posing for television cameras.

Mr. Kihss did not judge the committee one way or the other. He reported what Senator Welker wanted him to report—the increase of mail from Soviet sources, but he went on to suggest the need for Americans to read and study Soviet publications.

In the light of what goes on before a news story reaches print, of which the foregoing is only one illustration, the "objective" content analysis of finished news stories seems to miss the point so completely as to be as unreal as a game—a playing with words as with counters, with no regard for what they stand for or what was omitted before those particular words were chosen. Understanding the perceptual frameworks of those who supply the story and those who write and edit it is infinitely more important than staring at, counting, and other-wise analyzing the little black marks on paper that finally result. "The word is not the thing," we say. How true this is! And the news *report* is not the repor*ting*, which is a *process*—complex, perplexing, and human.[1]

Another view of writing problems is that "you can't write writing." Psychologist Wendell Johnson means by this that just as you can't read reading, one can only write about something. And that something is not words, but whatever those words represent. The first thing the student journalist must learn is that to communicate effectively his primary obligation is to be clear and understandable, not grammatically correct. Too often the student, because of training in English classes, bogs down by trying to write with ridiculous rules.

Johnson gives three main reasons for the failure of writing teachers:

[1] Ken Macrorie, "The Process of News Reporting," *The Use and Misuse of Language* (Fawcett Publications, Inc., 1962).

The first is that they do not appear to utilize to any considerable extent the principle of teaching by example. They tell the student how to write and how not to have written, but they don't, as a rule, do any actual writing for him or with him. They show him examples of what has been written, but no examples of something being written.

To try to learn to write by reading literature that has already been written and thoroughly jelled, instead of by observing the actual writing of literature, is much like trying to learn to bake a cake by eating one, instead of by watching the baker. One should teach by example, and what the teachers of English forget is that there are no examples of writing in the grammar book or the anthology; there are only generalized blueprints of statements yet unwritten and examples of something already written—cakes that were baked yesterday. The teacher herself has to provide the examples of writing to demonstrate the process. She must bake the cake of written English, not merely eat the cake that Hawthorne baked, as she stands before the class.

The second, and a more grave, reason for their failure is that they appear to place the emphasis on "writing," rather than on writing-about-something-for-someone. You cannot write writing. Or, at least if you do, you are not likely to learn how to write with clarity and validity, because they are not important to one who merely writes writing. Unless the emphasis is placed upon writing as a form of communication and directed very definitely, therefore, to an actual, live reader, the importance of clarity, organization, and validity is not likely to become very apparent. . . .

The third and final point in this "diagnosis" of English instruction is that teachers of English, with apparently only a few exceptions, cling tenaciously to two strange theories. The first is that writing is an art, and the second is that it cannot be taught. What they seem to mean when they say that writing is an art is that writing does not have to say anything—except to the reader who has "appreciation" —that writing is at its best when it is a form of expression *qua* expression.

In teaching the student to write, if one takes this view of "writing as an art," there is no point—in fact, there is a strong argument to the contrary—in training the student to express himself clearly or with validity. . . .

The explanation is extended when we recall the other theory, so popular among some teachers of English, that real effectiveness in writing, since it is an "art," cannot be taught at all. Only God can make a tree; the teacher of English can only water the tree with verbal dew in the hope of keeping it green, and even the value of doing that is debatable. . . .

And this pedagogical swooning by the teachers of English, on the theory that you can't make a silk purse out of a sow's ear, results in their making a great many sows' ears out of silk purses. It is not a question of the truth or falsity of their theory that effective writing cannot be taught, although this theory is probably not as largely true as many teachers of English suppose. The significant point is that the theory makes for unimaginative and lackadaisical teaching. Even God's trees might benefit from some systematic pruning and spraying.[1]

The journalism teacher has an excellent opportunity actually to demonstrate how a story is written, and he should invite professional journalists to show students how it is done. The second reason of failure is one that journalism overcomes; the student is assigned a story and has a waiting public. The third problem depends on the attitude of the teacher. Too often advisers fail to meet the challenge of improving the average writer. The strength of a staff at times depends on the ability of the average writer to improve. The teacher should encourage and aid this improvement for practical as well as ethical reasons.

Just as important as the writing problem is the right-wrong syndrome into which student journalists fall. Beginning students somehow try to state things in angel-devil, good-bad terms rather than the multivalued standpoint of the responsible press. *The New York Times* editorial may condemn Communism, but it attempts to see the other view. The Germans, Italians, and Japanese were our enemies in World War II but now are our friends, while our former friends, the Russians, Chinese, and French, appear to be hostile. There are people who object to this "shilly-shallying" and insist on a white-black judgment instead of the shades of gray that really color the majority of issues. The yes-

[1] Wendell Johnson, "You Can't Write Writing," *The Use and Misuse of Language* (New York: Fawcett Publications, Inc., 1962).

or-no group, as Hayakawa says, are the Gordian-knot cutters; they may undo the knot, but they ruin the rope. Students should realize this when writing blistering editorials about the "bad guys."

News sources sense when being interviewed into which category you have placed them. Honesty and empathy are two important traits of the good reporter. The empathic, non-evaluative reporter responds to a person's feelings as well as his words. Most of us think of a reply rather than really listening. Establishing rapport with a person usually leads to a better interview. Listening is an art that must be practiced by the student journalist. The quality of your information depends on your ability to listen to people. Like the fisherman, reporters often bemoan the loss of the story that got away. You have to listen to a story before you can write one.

Chapter 10

THE NEW JOURNALISM AND VALUES

> *The meaning of life here on*
> *earth might be defined as*
> *consisting in this: to unfold*
> *yourself, to work what thing you*
> *have the faculty for. It is a necessity*
> *for the human being, the first law*
> *of our existence.*
> —THOMAS CARLYLE

A sports writer said that when the television crews were on strike and management handled the cameras for a few days, he enjoyed watching a Boston Celtics basketball game far more than usual. The reason, he explained, was that only one camera was used and more overall "panning" or long-range shots were employed, allowing him to see more of the full-court action. He liked to see the play develop and the defensive reactions rather than concentrate on the individual player dribbling or shooting. Although the freshness of action and instant play-back have added a dimension for the viewing fan, the telephoto lens probably has been brought into too dominant a role at the sacrifice of overall coverage.

Curriculum revision currently going on in the United States suggests that we have been doing the same thing—engaging in too much specialization without concern for the whole of the discipline. The change in our society from absolutes to relatives in morality further separates the student from the teacher and the administration. The Space Age forced us to update science,

126

There are schools that already broadcast closed-circuit television news and sports programs for the students. The mass media are part of our lives, and the schools will soon have classes in news production for television. Photograph by San Bernardino Sun-Telegram.

math, English, and social studies. Journalism must keep pace in our pluralistic society, and the media is the message, not the medium, to paraphrase Marshall McLuhan, the controversial prophet of communications.

The Journalism Education Association has recognized this, albeit nearly a decade after the other disciplines. Elwood Karwand, JEA executive secretary, said:

It appears that we are going to recognize that journalism is a separate academic discipline and should be taught as such. Journalism is not English, social studies, psychology, sociology, speech or business, but rather cooperates with these disciplines in dealing with the world problems. We cannot separate the knowing from the doing. We cannot write unless we know something to write about, and we cannot communicate intelligently unless we have the skills necessary to make information meaningful. We must become more concerned about the relationship between today's high-school student and the mass media. Much of what he learns in today's classrooms will be left there. He may never again read Chaucer or Shakespeare, or listen to Beethoven or Bach, or recognize the worlds of Renoir or Raphael, but he will spend literally years with his newspapers and magazines or before his television set. These media will be his world of reality, and he must know how to deal with them, how to interpret them, and what to expect from them. The argument would surely be raised that this is not what should be, but the facts are that this is what happens today.

The "New Journalism" will require more of the teacher than ever before. The old lecture system must give way to the use of visual aids in the classroom. We are convinced that just anyone cannot teach the kind of journalism that our students deserve. School boards and administrators must be made more aware of the special skills and training that academic journalism demands.[1]

All too often a new faculty member who has had no journalism training is appointed publications adviser. And the students he finds are often the misfits that the counselor could not pigeon-

---

[1] Elwood Karwand, "JEA Notes," *Scholastic Editor,* January 1966.

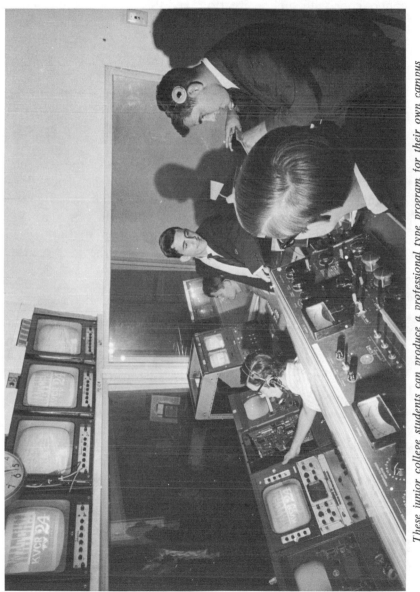

These junior college students can produce a professional type program for their own campus community. Video replays of campus events will insure students seeing entertainment, news, and sports before school, during lunch, and after school. Photograph by San Bernardino Sun-Telegram.

hole elsewhere. Journalism has far too long been a dumping ground and a second choice in the curriculum. The new adviser cannot cope with such a situation, and this is how a cycle starts. Principals also feel more secure by selecting "little old ladies" who are not likely to "make waves." This is also the reason why administrators fear the football coach who is too successful—he becomes a threat. Yet the coach is chosen on the basis of his ability to teach football, and the same rule should apply to the publications adviser. The principal backs the team by appearing at games, and he should do the same for the publication by reading it and by meeting with the staff.

No studies are available to evaluate the needs of the students. The surveys made are simply projections for the demand of current positions. Curriculum design should include investigation of student capabilities and interest in the mass media. We should not simply guess at the learning potential, but try to measure and estimate the quality and level of the new courses needed.

PRINCIPALS' PRINCIPLES

Three high-school principals commented on the values of publications during a symposium. W. J. Farmer of Triadelphia High School in Wheeling, West Virginia, said that journalism comes closer to fulfilling the integral part-of-the-instruction objective than does any other of the school's forty organized extra-class activities.

Publication is actually an extension of the formal curriculum—a laboratory where what a student learns from a teacher can be tried out on a mass audience.

Perhaps a principal is more interested in and critical of publications than of any other activity. He is demanding because he recognizes that publications are a tremendous vehicle for desirable community relations. He knows that they can exert tremendous influences in leadership of the student body. He is aware that they provide an outlet and incentive for creative writing and that publications should teach the virtues of honesty, reliability, integrity, and leadership.

Clifford O. Brake of Buckhannon-Upshur High School in Buckhannon, West Virginia, outlined five purposes that justify school publications:

(1) To acquaint students with the state and national community through exchange papers, yearbooks, seminars, workshops, press conferences.

(2) To establish proper business attitudes by establishing a budget, planning sales and advertising campaigns to raise money, and keeping the cost of the publication within the budget limit.

(3) To establish a friendly working relationship with local newspapers.

(4) To develop a sense of citizenship responsibility toward the school community in the accurate collection and disbursement of news.

(5) To break the barriers of provincialism, by sending students to workshops on University campuses when possible.

Brake went on to cite measuring devices that can be used to gauge what should be included in a publication:

(1) Information included should be true.

(2) The material included should not cause embarrassment.

(3) Everything in the paper should be in good taste.

(4) The different points of view printed in the paper should be constructive rather than destructive.

(5) Nonsense should be excluded—this does not mean that wholesome humor should be excluded.

Brake said that after having determined the educational objectives and fitted the publications policies within the framework, the administration should do a thorough job of assisting the publication. He listed provision of materials, suitable working place, and time in the school schedule as some of the ways in which the administrator can contribute to the success of a publication.

Paul G. Michael of East Fairmont High School, Fairmont, West Virginia, cites both values and responsibilities as seen by a principal:

I. Sees values

  a. To student
1. Training in communications skills
2. Experience in teamwork, diplomacy
3. Aid in finding a place in school life (adjusting)
4. Opportunity for practical use of skills derived from other classes

  b. To school system
1. Creation of school spirit, morals, etc.
2. Public relations value—news bureau
3. A record for handy reference—yearbook; or for historical purposes—paper

II. Has responsibilities

  a. To student
1. Stimulates interest in journalism work
2. Schedules classes so that few conflicts arise with required courses
3. Provides atmosphere conducive to publications
4. Displays confidence in and backs the staff

  b. To teacher
1. Helps instructor interest students in journalism
2. Relieves instructor of other extracurricular duties to provide time for work on publications
3. Urges instructor to become qualified to do publications work
4. Provides place to work and good equipment to work with

  c. To the school system
1. Publicizes value of journalism in curriculum
2. Inspires cooperation among staffs, faculties, other schools, public, etc.
3. Demands respect, fair play, and loyalty
4. Balances journalism with other school areas[1]

[1] The three principals participated in a 1965 Newspaper Fund Workshop at West Virginia University in a symposium on "The School Administration and Publications Policy."

ADVISER'S VIEWS

Former adviser Donna Barnhill said that administrators and counselors seem unaware of the value of journalism skills.

They generally regard them as necessary for getting out the school newspaper or the yearbook, or for training future journalists. However, journalism is a highly specialized profession. High-school pupils are no more prepared to enter this profession after work on a school newspaper than they are to enter medical practice on the basis of a biology course. Students can't be expected to master the intricacies of style and form of news stories in one or two elective courses.

To a larger group of students in our consumer society, journalism serves as a practical humanities course along with perfecting, in a painless operation, the tools of communication—spelling, grammar, punctuation, language flexibility, and expressiveness. Moreover, apart from its academic value, journalism is an aid to social, personality, and character development. What more could one ask from a public school course? [1]

Perhaps one of the problems in journalism is that a student *can* get a job on a professional newspaper after just a course or two. Journalism is perhaps the only profession left that is not licensed. No minimum standards are set. After more than a half-century of hiring reporters off the street at wages well below that of the supermarket box boy, newspapers are finding that the talent well is running dry. Wages are becoming more competitive, and publishers now realize that a college-trained reporter will have a far greater chance of staying than the here-today, gone-tomorrow reporter of the past. Very few papers can afford to keep on training newcomers, much less pay the penalty that a high staff turnover causes. Publishers rationalize this by claiming that the top reporters had a place to start and were not held back. In reality, many newcomers have dropped out of the newspaper profession to enter public relations or advertising instead of moving up the newspaper ladder. Somewhere between the

[1] Donna Barnhill, "Many Values Are Derived from School Publications," *The Clearing House,* May 1965.

secondary schools and the jobs, students have reconsidered their professional futures. Salaries have been a major factor in these decisions, but the money gap has been narrowed in recent years under the old law of supply and demand.

The values and rewards of student publications are growing greater as it becomes even more important to understand the mass media and to be able to communicate clearly and accurately. Publication training is the first step toward awareness of mass communications. The New Journalism will take the second step of including electronic journalism in the curriculum that now stresses print journalism, which has often failed to include advertising, propaganda, news magazines, and semantics.

Ability to take notes and summarize a speech are invaluable to students in college lecture classes. Learning how to interview persons, knock on doors, and investigate a story has always appealed to students.

Journalism should be "where the action is," to use the current term. Although salaries were mentioned as one of the reasons for the decline of reporting as a career, the prime reason could be the shift toward the Peace Corps and War on Poverty by idealistic students. Somewhere along the line newspapers lost the crusading spirit that attracted bright young students regardless of the pay. The materialism of the 1950's caused students to look for security, and this led them to public relations and allied fields. The crusaders of the 1960's turned to civil rights and involvement in politics as exemplified by President Kennedy. Students made the news rather than reporting it. The mood has shifted with the Hippie Revolution as a non-intellectual revolt away from the center of the campus. The underground press produced by this movement is far different from the Free Speech Movement of Mario Savio at the University of California. The Flower Power protests over Vietnam, drugs, LSD, sex, love, and money have spilled over into the secondary schools, just as the civil-rights techniques shifted to the Vietnam peace marches.

Problems of switching over to the New Journalism in the schools might be solved by flexible scheduling. This would allow the teacher to divide a course into lecture and lab sections. Five one-hour periods per week are not practical for journalism. Two one-hour lecture periods and a two- or three-hour lab section would accomplish far more, since students need the longer time for writing and editing. The frequency of the publication should decide scheduling.

Another suggestion is that basic communications theory and the study of the mass media become a standard unit in English curricula, perhaps three weeks on communications in the 10th grade and three weeks on mass media in the 11th grade. The Now Generation has already been "turned on" by electronic media; they still need to understand it. The New Journalism should teach the carry-over communications values that today's youth need to survive the media fallout.

Chapter 11

UNDERSTANDING MEDIA

> *The Medium Is the Message*
> —MARSHALL MCLUHAN

We live, as one critic said, in an age of overwrite and under-think. The problem of selectivity is becoming more challenging as the mass media try to drown us in a torrent of information. Yet capturing an idea in a cage of words will probably be as frustrating to student journalists in the future as it is now. Just as a spearfisherman has to make allowances for the way in which water distorts his vision, the reporter must realize that the language he writes pulls reality out of shape. Too often we communicate in meaningless clichés and attach social significance to grammar. This triteness and snobbishness is a barrier to efficient reporting.

The chapter on the New Journalism briefly mentioned how the mass media would have to be included. The student journalist has not really learned to use pictures to the fullest, much less magazines, radio, television, paperbacks, and films. There seem to be signs of a growing magazine movement in the schools, and this offers a promising format for future student journalists. Many junior colleges in California have dropped the traditional yearbook in favor of a quarterly or semesterly magazine. Actually, a news magazine offers the best medium for the secondary-school message. Such a magazine would include literary works and be a High School Illustrated publication. The price would have to be raised to cover production costs and slicker paper, but the results would make it worthwhile. A senior edition at

136

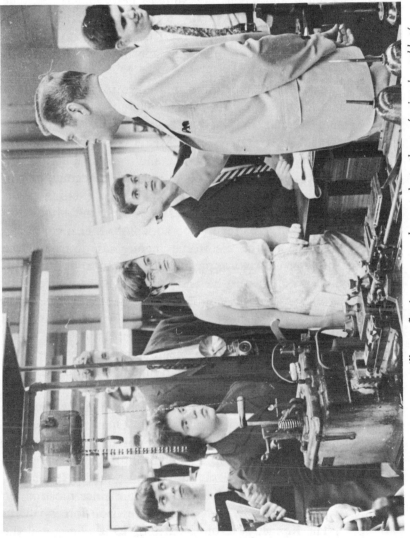

Tours of newspapers are still an effective way to show students the professional world of communications. Field trips are a necessity in any journalism program.

the end of the year could include graduation activities and pictures of the classes. Thus the yearbook could be eliminated. Don't be alarmed, however; the majority of schools will retain yearbooks even if and when they shift to news magazines. The increasing costs of yearbooks may force new schools to start a new tradition—the news magazine. I used to tell my students that a tradition was often a mistake made many years ago that had not been corrected.

Student journalists of the future may have to cope with what Marshall McLuhan calls Mixed Media, where the image is multiplied, fragmented, and combined with a sound that is also multiplied and fragmented. The Mixed Media avoids the "linear" thought imposed by the print media and is aimed at the TV generation. The screen as well as the music has become stereo. One critic predicts that the multiple picture has exciting possibilities for education. That is still far beyond the Gutenberg Galaxy. What is the media revolution about? As McLuhan points out, the challenge of the electronic media has destroyed the monopoly of the printed word, particularly in education. In order to understand media, it must be understood that the written language mutes all senses except sight and the focus is on one thing at a time, thus making it linear. In oral language, the eye hears and the ear sees. The electronic media has caused this to be simultaneous. By saying that the medium is the message, McLuhan means that a totally new environment has been created. Yet the content of this new medium is the medium of the film, just as when writing was formed, the old oral dialogues became the content of the new medium—the book. One example of the medium as the message is that Eskimos carve, then throw the art away. With the current crop-dusting of information, the classroom must become the civil defense against media fallout, as one critic put it. Reading is a passive medium, since most of the thinking is done for you by the writer. Television forces you to participate. The Kennedy-Nixon debates of 1960 eliminated the newspaper as a major political force in national elections. The middleman was eliminated and the voters now decide after a multisensory appraisal. The new media are not being properly taught in the schools today, and the student journalist and adviser must take the responsibility of leading journalism into an expanded discipline. The Electric World is battling the Literate-Visual World for supremacy with the student. Just look at the hippies and you know who is winning. McLuhan thinks that the theater per se is dead. Yet we teach drama and not the New Media to our students. Two good works to read about the media battle are *Understanding Media: The Extensions of Man* by McLuhan and *Using Mass Media in the Schools,* edited by William D. Boutwell.

Father John M. Culkin of Fordham University is leading the fight to make film an acceptable medium in the schools. He points out that "too often tedium is the message" in education. The average high-school student, he says, has 15,000 hours of television viewing behind him by the time he graduates. He wants to bring motion pictures into the classroom and let the student become a critic. And the student journalist of today could even produce his own film with some of the low-cost equipment now available. The final test in the classroom will be for the student journalists to produce newscasts, documentaries, and feature films. Script writing is one of the best-paying jobs today, but schools are still training students for only one medium. Culkin also warns that school can ruin film by giving it the Beowulf-to-Salinger treatment and having multiple-choice questions on screen tests.

McLuhan has some rather controversial opinions about the relationship of the press and mass media:

> The massive theme of the press can be managed only by direct contact with the formal patterns of the medium in question. It is thus necessary to state at once that "human interest" is a technical term meaning that which happens when multiple book pages or multiple information items are arranged in a mosaic on one sheet. The book is a private confessional form that provides a "point of view." The press is a group confessional form that provides communal participation. It can "color" events by using them or by not using them

at all. But it is the daily communal exposure of multiple items in juxtaposition that gives the press its complex dimension of human interest.

The book form is not a communal mosaic or corporate image but a private voice. One of the unexpected effects of TV on the press has been a great increase in the popularity of *Time* and *Newsweek*. Quite inexplicably to themselves and without any new effort at subscription, their circulations have more than doubled since TV. These news magazines are preeminently mosaic in form, offering not windows on the world like the old picture magazines, but presenting corporate images of society in action. Whereas the spectator of a picture magazine is passive, the reader of a news magazine becomes much involved in the making of meanings for the corporate image. Thus the TV habit of involvement in mosaic image has greatly strengthened the appeal of these news magazines, but at the same time has diminished the appeal of the older pictorial feature magazines.

Both book and newspaper are confessional in character, creating the effect of *inside story* by their mere form, regardless of content. As the book page yields the inside story of the author's mental adventures, so the press page yields the inside story of the community in action and interaction. It is for this reason that the press seems to be performing its function most when revealing the seamy side. Real news is bad news—bad news *about* somebody, or bad news *for* somebody. In 1962, when Minneapolis had been for months without a newspaper, the chief of police said: "Sure, I miss the news, but so far as my job goes I hope the papers never come back. There is less crime around without a newspaper to pass around the ideas."

The classified ads (and stock-market quotations) are the bedrock of the press. Should an alternative source of easy access to such diverse daily information be found, the press will fold. Radio and TV can handle the sports, news, comics, and pictures.

The editorial, which is the one book-feature of the newspaper, has been ignored for many years, unless put in the form of news or paid advertisement. . . .

A friend of mine who tried to teach something about the forms of media in secondary school was struck by one unanimous response. The students could not for a moment accept the suggestion that the press or any other public means of communication could be used with base intent. They felt that this would be akin to polluting the air or the water supply, and they didn't feel that their friends and relatives employed in these media would sink to such corruption. Failure in perception occurs precisely in giving attention to the program "content" of our media while ignoring the form, whether it be radio or print or the English language itself. There have been countless Newton Minows (formerly head of the Federal Communications Commission) to talk about the Wasteland of the Media, men who know nothing about the form of any medium whatever. They imagine that a more earnest tone and a more austere theme would pull up the level of the book, the press, the movie, and TV. They are wrong to a farcical degree. They have only to try out their theory for fifty consecutive words in the mass medium of the English language. What would Mr. Minow do, what would any advertiser do, without the well-worn and corny clichés of popular speech? Suppose that we were to try for a few sentences to raise the level of our daily English conversation by a series of sober and serious sentiments? Would this be a way of getting at the problems of improving the medium? If all English were enunciated at a Mandarin level of uniform elegance and sententiousness, would the language and its users be better served? [1]

You may not agree with the controversial prophet from Canada, but you certainly can't ignore him. The student journalist and adviser will have to be aware of and understand the problems of the New Media. One of the goals of scholastic journalism is to produce students who can communicate—and this has to include the electronic media.

[1] Marshall McLuhan, *Understanding Media: The Extensions of Man.* New York: McGraw-Hill Book Company, 1965.

Chapter 12

CONTESTS: CON & PRO

> I am leader: therefore I
> must follow.
>
> —VOLTAIRE

How much advising should an adviser do? Can you compare *The New York Times* with your hometown daily or weekly? Should you? In a society that demands winners, what is the place of contests in student publications?

My first experience as an adviser made me realize that, unlike the sport coach, I could play the game for my students. Because of my background in both scholastic and professional journalism, students took it for granted that I would take a dominant role in the production of the newspaper and the annual. But I didn't. My role was to advise the students, not do the work. Before and after issues I would advise, but during production I tried to let students solve their own problems. The editor had to worry about the headlines that were long, the stories that were short, the pictures that were the wrong size, and the typographical errors made by the gremlins. When the newspaper won several awards, other advisers winked and said I had an unfair advantage because of my background. They didn't believe I used a hands-off policy except in an emergency. My philosophy is that after the first quarter the staff should virtually run the show and the senior editors should have enough experience to handle the problems. Some advisers point a staff toward contests and even print a couple of late copies after corrections just to enter in contests.

There are several reasons for a publication to enter contests.

Awards can help motivate students and demonstrate that someone cares about excellence at their level. A display of such awards helps build pride and tradition in a publication.

One is to obtain another view of your product; a second is to get a comparison with similar schools. When someone else blows your horn, the prestige is much more meaningful than when you do it. Another objective is to reward students and not just the publication. The On-The-Spot writing tournaments sponsored by the Journalism Education Association in California are an outstanding example of rewarding individual students. Students compete in news, editorial, features, and sports categories, with the presentation and judging (by professionals) done in one day. This is an incentive for the outstanding student who feels that financial or other handicaps prevent the publication from winning awards; it gives him a chance to compete as an individual. Since the writing is done without help, there is no question of major editing changes being made by an adviser or other person. In addition to writing, contests of this type can be held for headlines, captions, photography, makeup, advertising, and editing.

The problem with many contests is that the criteria are very subjective. *The New York Times* has no comics and its makeup is 100 years behind the times, and yet it is rated the foremost newspaper in the nation. It wouldn't make the top ten in a national scholastic contest! Some student papers are penalized because they do not carry advertising. Others are penalized because they carry advertising on the editorial page to equalize the ad line. The socio-economic conditions of a school often dictate the financial status of the publication, yet contests consider only number of students, type of printing, and frequency of publication. One way to get a higher rating is to drop from weekly to monthly publication; this quadruples the time for writing and editing copy, yet it is not a realistic publishing schedule.

Another problem is the negative aspects of contests. A second-class rating can destroy staff morale just as surely as an All-American rating can inspire students. What has happened in student publication contests is that only the "winners" keep competing. The publications with consistently low ratings, whatever the reason, usually drop out. And yet they are often the ones that need help the most. Some contests have been based on self-improvement from one year to the next, yet this penalizes the consistently good publication.

Although the adviser cannot do much about the national contests, many types of local contests can be extremely helpful. Local newspaper publishers and press clubs are taking increasing interest in sponsoring best-of-the-year awards for individual schools. Although it is not used much, competition on the league level, as in sports, is another way to stimulate students to put out a better product. Ask your area publishers to contribute $100 or more a year for each school contest and perhaps a similar prize for first place in a league contest for best newspaper and yearbook.

The yearbook problem is slightly different. Many sophisticated yearbook companies now move in and virtually put out a book themselves. A professional artist and photographer, plus layout designer and binder, take the book out of the hands of the students except for captions and copy. How can you rate such a production?

One of the major contests recently defended itself against an attack. Here is how *Scholastic Editor* sees the problem:

We're putting out our book (paper) for the students and not for contest judges.

This is a familiar line to yearbook and newspaper judges at National Scholastic Press Association and, we dare guess, at the other major critical services—Columbia Scholastic Press Association, Quill
· & Scroll, and Catholic Scholastic Press Association.

What the line usually means is that staff and/or adviser preferred to take the easy way out (trivia, baby pictures, class wills, gossip columns, senior snapshots, all the other junk that tarnishes so with time). It's harder to put out a good book or paper, one that will have real meaning to the student tomorrow as well as today. Edmund Arnold put it beautifully in his new book on yearbooks, when he said that *to freeze time successfully, the staff needs complete coverage, the highest quality of word and picture, impeccable accuracy.* . . . The idea is just as applicable to newspapers as to yearbooks.

When asked to answer the question—for students or judges?—

NSPA's standard answer is that what the judges want and what the standards demand is a book or paper that is truly good for the students, that will give them what they will find useful, valuable, and meaningful. No one can really argue against completeness, quality, and accuracy.

From the staff member or adviser who would rather rationalize than work for quality, the comment is expectable and understandable. But such a comment is neither expectable or understandable from someone who ought to know better. It is particularly painful when he then goes on to advocate the same basic ideas, to insist upon the same general excellence, completeness, quality, and accuracy that the major critical services have urged for years.

It's rather like one doctor telling you to disregard what another doctor told you, then giving essentially the same advice all over again. Two such cases came up recently.

In an article in the NEA *Journal,* February, 1967, Chris Steers, associate professor of journalism, Miami-Dade (Fla.) Junior College, says *let's give students what they want. . . .* The professor says formats have become *stereotyped as schools conformed to the standards of the national judging competitions* and blames this for what is described as a funless, boring book. The professor's solution: . . . *give the book back to all the students. Get the average kids into it. Show them in their classes . . . more and better copy . . . more than a compilation of varsity scores, a listing of prom queens, and so on. . . . A yearbook that says little or nothing about the exciting things that took place in the education process at the school leaves a big void. . . .*

Professor Steers wrote more, but you'll find the same basic ideas urged in the NSPA Guidebook and expressed in All American yearbooks. That's why they made All American.

Mr. Arnold writes in his new book that judges *seem to see themselves as guardians of tradition . . . but you can console yourself with the truth that you are producing a book for your readers, not for some distant judge.* Were one to apply the same techniques of measuring value of advice by distance instead of quality, one would also probably have to reject the advice of the distant teacher (i.e., Mr. Arnold), and this would be patently absurd. Mr. Arnold is probably the best typographer in the field today. And unquestionably one of the best teachers.

What is saddening is the generalization that critical services are to blame for all the ills of yearbooks and newspapers today, that they have been holding back staffs and advisers. For decades the critical services have been preaching the gospel of completeness, quality, and accuracy. Isn't it just as logical to give the critical services credit for all the achievements of publications?

NSPA is not and should not be immune to criticism. Nor should the other critical services be. But elementary fairness demands just a little better shake.

The all-inclusive, blanket condemnation of critical services as keepers of the flame of the past has implicitly in it an idea that we find hard to swallow: That All American publications—and other top-rated ones, too—must therefore be examples of antiquity.

We don't think these publications are rejected by their readers as something archaic. We urge those who do to try reading some of the All Americans.[1]

An even stronger plea in behalf of national ratings has been made by an adviser-judge. Incidentally, many advisers become judges just so they can benefit by the exchanges and knowledge of the criteria. It should be stressed that the newspaper and yearbook contests have to be evaluated differently. Although they have shortcomings, they do provide another view, and many times staffs will listen to the "expert" from afar although you may have said the same thing previously.

Here is a view on yearbook contests:

Why enter the critical services? It's only one judge's opinion and every judge goes by different rules. . . . We don't care about ratings. They mean nothing . . . we want to please our students along with the administration. . . . If we don't receive a higher rating, we shall never again enter this contest! . . . All judges are prejudiced.

These are a few of the choice items which judges read, hear, and face each year. The complaints elaborated above illustrate the one basic fact which far too many advisers and editors overlook: As in every phase of life, there are rules, and if anyone does not wish to

[1] Kathleen K. Leabo, "The Editor Speaks . . .", *Scholastic Editor*, April 1967.

regard the rules of any specific contest, the book from his school should not be entered.

Apparently, too many advisers and staff members are also forgetting the prime purpose of the yearbook . . . to report completely and factually the history of one entire year at their school.

The basic purpose for any critical service seems clearly to be to help each adviser and editor *see* his publication through the eyes of a judge who examines *many* yearbooks and who goes by a set of *suggestions*.

How many students know the principles of good journalism when they tackle the job of publishing a yearbook? (How many students *know* Shakespeare the day they walk into class, or how many teachers allow their students to select only what they want to learn?) How many advisers have been *pushed* into the job and wish only to *put out a yearbook?* But how many staffs and advisers want to publish a real yearbook, even though they may lack the basic knowledge to do a genuine job for the school?

Take the initial step to good journalism and obtain a booklet from each of the three major critical services—National Scholastic Press Association, Columbia Scholastic Press Association and National School Yearbook Association. Southern schools should also write for a copy of Southern Interscholastic Press Association's booklet.

Points allocated for each category may vary; the weight placed on various phases of the yearbook may differ, but each basically resembles the other. Yes, judges may interpret the manner of execution differently, but in eleven years of advising a yearbook and in having it judged in four different critical services, only once in 44 times has a judge differed in the overall rating of our book.

Indeed, some critical services maintain the same judge for two or three years in the same category in order for him to judge the progress of a specific group of books. Writing now as a judge, far too often those hours of work (even up to five per book) seem to have been ignored. The staffs fail to study the principles as listed in the guidebook and they have failed in their duty to serve their school more effectively and to give it and the students a true history of the year.

Let's go back to 1956, my first year as a green adviser for our yearbook. The copy sounded like a student guidebook or catalog. There were no headlines to tie the story of the year together. Not one action shot dispelled the formality of the organizations. Cropped pictures just did not exist and every layout employed one of the principles which would have made the book great in the late 1930's. Student life? There simply was not a picture to show that life existed at Augusta.

How did this happen? How could it occur? First, the staff was new at the task. Second, the adviser had not worked on a yearbook since the 1940's. Third, *knowledge* of the critical services' guidebooks and magazines was totally missing. So the staff and adviser eagerly put out a publication which was roasted in each of the services.

Determined was the group which gathered the next fall. A composite was made of each suggestion from the judges, and even though the adviser and the staff literally bled, the group dedicated itself to publish a more literate edition the following year.

Although the results were far from complete, the judges apparently recognized a genuine attempt at following the *rules* of good journalism. Most important, the students were delighted to see their names in complete captions with every picture in the book and the school officials were proud of the achievement in presenting more thorough coverage of the school year.

Such terms, however, as inner margins, complete classroom coverage, balance in layout, use of verticals and well-cropped pictures, though mentioned in the guidebooks and in the criticisms, were not understood by the staff and adviser. Too often experts forget that staffs are so new that a more thorough explanation is needed.

As staffs began to learn more, yearbook services became more specific. They, too, changed; each one began to elaborate on the *meanings* of certain elusive terms. Each subsequent staff learned more as such books as Allnutt's, Medlin's, Lloyd's, Magmer's and Spencer's were acquired and studied carefully by each person on the staff.

The school officials learned the value of having an award-winning yearbook, but the sweetest sounds came from the students as they proudly showed *their* yearbooks to parents, relatives, friends, and dates. Once a student photographer failed to take pictures on registration day. The superintendent was far more concerned than was the adviser!

Rules change as photo-journalism advances as a technique of reporting. Revisions of guidebooks are more frequent, and each year the staff and adviser discover that each must be studied more completely. New books, new magazine articles, and new pamphlets furnish far more information than was available a mere ten years ago.

One adviser wrote recently, *Our classroom time is a sacred time and no pictures may be taken.* This is true—the classroom is important—and if the principal does ban the camera during class hours, then the adviser can certainly arrange for various phases of the different subject areas to be photographed after class hours.

The adviser *must* understand that curriculum coverage in headlines, copy, photographs, and captions is a necessity in every yearbook today if the yearbook is to cover the full history of one year. The value to the school and to the students may not seem obvious today, but ten years from now, it will be. Take a check on the yearbook of ten years ago in your school; see what its value is.

Our students want only cute sayings. This may seem true, but if this is a dire necessity, let this be the introduction to a complete caption which paints a word picture for the reader. *Our students want to create a mood. We don't want any captions, headlines, or copy.* This merely indicates a lazy staff and an even lazier adviser! A picture needs words to pinpoint the mood.

Our students don't read copy. Indeed, this is the absolute truth—when the copy is so poor that it is a mere handbook and not a lively, youthful, enthusiastic, gleeful reporting of what happened THIS year. Many students don't read every word at once, but students whose yearbooks receive top ratings (those books in which the copy flows) DO read the copy carefully in the entire book. An error here or there in reporting is NEVER overlooked by eager readers.

I can remember a delightful adviser from Atlanta who smarted under a score of 621 (out of 1,000) in one contest. For five hours she went over the book with the judge. She entered her book in every service the following year and purchased suggested texts, and in three years her book was an All American, Medalist and a trophy winner. The feat was repeated the following year and the 1966 edition was even better! Sales soared from below 50 percent to 90.

It can be done. Even in one year. A local high school just published a yearbook which is fantastic. A glance at the 1965 edition and then one at the 1966 copy illustrates that ever popular comment, *Would you believe?* The staff and adviser learned the rules and techniques of good journalism, and the entire student body is elated over the change.

Certainly it takes work, devotion, and a GOAL. It takes a youthful spirit, but it also requires that criticism be taken fairly and that self-analysis be made. It should be done if the yearbook is to reflect the times, the changes, the history of one complete year in the life of a school and its people.

So now, let's start on a real improvement program. This really places a task on the adviser, for he MUST become an authority. Study the guidebooks carefully, and if a point in the book or in the criticism is not clear, write the judge or the critical service.

It should be clear now. Every book should be entered in critical services for the education of the staff in the techniques of good journalism in order to serve better the school, the students, and the community.[1]

I feel that contests are usually overrated. The adviser knows who is actually doing the work and whether the staff is working up to capability. A new adviser would benefit most from evaluations, but it is disheartening to the newcomer when financial or other reasons result in a poor rating for a staff that is really trying. Don't try to aim your publication for the contests—you have to serve the school first.

[1] Colonel C. E. Savedge, "Are Yearbook Judges Prejudiced?", *Scholastic Editor*, June 1967.

Chapter 13

EVALUATION AND FEEDBACK

> Quality is never an accident. It is
> always the result of intelligent
> effort. There must be the will to
> produce a superior thing.
>   —JOHN RUSKIN

Since the first school newspapers were published in the early 1800's, advisers have been facing the problem of evaluating students and publications. National contests have already been discussed, but not the reporter and his product. Does everyone on the staff earn a "letter" each year? Can a typist earn an A in journalism? Should you hold a critique for each story and edition? How do you know the content of your publication is appropriate? What feedback are you getting from students, faculty, and administration?

When I was a reporter on my high-school paper we received a grade for each story, but the semester mark was determined by total inches. Headlines and captions each counted one inch and we were required to keep a "string" of all printed stories. There was no real quality factor, although one misspelled name in a story would mean a D and two an F. Sports writers and feature writers often win the Inch Derby because their stories are usually longer. I favor a weekly report that would include stories assigned and written plus other work done, such as editing, typing, makeup, photography. If you require use of carbons, this provides an excellent method to go over pre-edited copy. Each student should have a folder with weekly reports filed after a short

152

When professionals visit your class and discuss journalism with students, a contact is made that quite often motivates a student to enter the profession. Advisers should try to have at least one such speaker per quarter. Photograph by Coates Crewe.

conference with the adviser. Some advisers don't feel that a student should receive a journalism grade for typing or "leg" work (the latter refers to running down stories, not cheesecake posing). The football coach letters the waterboy, and a newspaper is similar to a team in that members contribute varying talents to insure success. Business, advertising, and circulation are part of the world of professional as well as scholastic journalism, a fact that academic-minded advisers often forget.

Many advisers dislike criticizing stories or editions, yet improvement is geared to learning from mistakes. The personality of the adviser and of the student must be taken into consideration. Some advisers make the criticism seem personal and sarcastic. How do you evaluate the story and not have the student feel that his own integrity is also being rated? I learned in the "chew 'em out" school of journalism, but I don't recommend it today. Just as the half-time oration has been replaced by objective appraisal of performance by football coaches, the adviser must utilize other methods. One method may be using the overhead or opaque projector to illustrate errors. Another may be to have the student editors meet with reporters, so that ratings come from a peer. The editors, of course, may have to be briefed. Advisers do not always have time to talk to students individually, and group sessions are usually better for certain types of problems. I liked to have a "razz sheet" of each edition marked for staff meetings. Praise is just as important, and good makeup, heads, leads, and photos should always be pointed out. Posting the best headlines of the week can also spur competition among the editors. Many professional newspapermen will gladly evaluate editions and discuss them with the staff. This is much better than national contests, because the local journalist learns about the problems of scholastic publishing while the students have a chance to defend their work.

Too often beginning advisers bog down over style errors in evaluation. The quality of the writing and the depth of the story are much more important. High-school audiences are much more sophisticated today, and student publications should reflect this trend. The skills, attitudes, and knowledge that are required for student journalists should be written out. These standards should be clear enough and high enough for the students to grasp the goals and objectives of the course. Many problems could be avoided by more careful screening of prospective students. A student's desire to be sports editor isn't enough to warrant his selection. Yearbook staffs in particular should establish criteria for positions that can be tested. Some advisers bemoan having to bail out a weak editor when a major share of the blame can be laid to poor selection. The post-Sputnik emphasis on math and science in the past decade may have hurt elective courses such as journalism.

A survey[1] in southern California shows that although quality is on the upswing in junior-college and college journalism, secondary-school classes have shown a steady downward trend. Most teachers cited higher entrance requirements and greater competition to get into the top colleges as reasons for students' bypassing journalism in favor of English and other academic courses. To compound the problem, counselors fill the journalism classes with dropouts from physics or with problem students. Small classes are not allowed in most crowded high schools, and unless the adviser has the right to approve all staff members, misfits are sent. Some administrators do not want strong journalism programs and will not take the necessary steps to insure a successful publication. Thus the adviser should provide counselors with minimum standards, and these should encompass more than the usual B or better in English. Many excellent journalists are employed today who earned only C's in English. Recruiting from junior-high staffs and holding a yearly writing contest open to all students are other methods of finding potential writers.

Two other factors previously mentioned that can reverse this downward trend are flexible scheduling and a more comprehen-

[1] David C. Henley, "Journalism Education in Southern California," *Monthly Bulletin* of Los Angeles County Schools Office, January 1966.

sive communications course. The former would allow students to take more electives; the latter would probably be considered an academic subject, which the present journalism course is not in California. Regardless of these problems, the adviser must have a method for selecting the student and another for evaluating his improvement.

SCHOLASTIC FEEDBACK

Few professional newspapers keep up to date as to what the public wants to read. Newspapers fought television for years, then found that their readers wanted TV guides and stories about the medium. What about the scholastic press? Is your publication's antenna receiving only the principal and the student council? Some 55 high-school student editors at a Wisconsin journalism workshop were polled about journalism and had some interesting responses.[1]

The students rated Vietnam and civil rights as the two most important concerns of the time. But within the school environment, lunchroom conditions were the major concern. Some 27 of the 55 editors named the cafeteria a hot issue, with complaints ranging from poor food and excessive prices to crowded conditions and too-short lunch periods. School policies and dress and hair regulations were second and third, and student freedom was fourth. Limitation of student-government power and inadequate curriculum and instructional quality followed. Homework and school spirit, two common gripes, were far down the list.

Only one editor said he had no control over editorials; 10 said they had some control, 30 said they had control a greater part of the time, and 10 said they had complete freedom. But this may be misleading, since one student said that the adviser selected appropriate editorial subjects at the beginning of the year. What is needed for comparison is a survey of how the students at those same 55 schools would have reacted to the same poll.

[1] Alan Bussel and James M. Force, "Fledgling Editors Present Opinions on Media, World," *Editor & Publisher,* August 12, 1967.

CONTENT ANALYSIS OF 25 CATEGORIES OF NEWS AND READER
EVALUATIONS OF IMPORTANCE AND INTEREST IN 35 ISSUES OF THE
DAILY BRUIN

Rank Order of Total Inches	Category	% of Total Inches Allo-cated	% of Positive Reader Responses			
			Importance		Interest	
			Rank	%	Rank	%
1	Major sports	16.8	6	88	14	68
2	Letters	13.3	9	86	4	84
3	Student government	7.1	6	88	17	58
4	Students—individual	6.9	19	68	15	60
5	Editorials	6.8	13	85	9	77
6	Women's news	6.7	24	33	24	30
7	General coverage	6.6	3	92	3	86
8	Intellectual activity	5.5	1	97	2	87
9	Fraternities—dorms	3.8	21	58	20	40
10	Schools—departments	3.3	8	87	11	71
11	Extra-curricular—social	3.1	9	86	12	70
12	Social—political	2.7	9	86	4	84
13	Faculty—individual	2.5	3	92	8	78
14	Administration	2.2	3	92	6	83
15	Cultural events	2.0	2	95	1	88
16	Minor sports	1.9	20	63	22	37
17	Other universities	1.7	15	78	7	80
18	Other news	1.6				
19	Intramural sports	1.5	22	57	21	38
20	Religious news	1.5	23	50	23	34
21	Physical campus	1.4	18	75	12	70
22	Honorary—academic	.8	14	80	18	56
23	Faculty—senate	.3	9	86	16	59
24	Special projects	.0 +	17	76	19	45
25	Columns	.0	16	77	10	72

A revealing content analysis of a college newspaper has been
made by two journalism professors at the University of California
at Los Angeles.[1] Their survey of 35 issues of the *Daily Bruin* re-

[1] Jack Lyle and Walter Wilcox. *Students View the News—The Daily Bruin Study* (UCLA Department of Journalism Series, 1962).

sulted from criticism that the editors were antifraternity, immature, politically biased, and were giving poor coverage to campus events.

The responses indicated that the editors overestimated the interest in sports and underestimated the interest in four categories of more serious news. This type of feedback is necessary if scholastic journalism is going to do more than fly by the seat of its pants. This does not mean that surveys should rule, but rather that such tools should be considered in deciding the content of the publication. Offhand remarks and casual observations may be giving editors very erroneous ideas about the job they are doing. There are more dangers in not making such surveys than in doing so.

Evaluation and feedback are increasingly important problems for student journalists and advisers to face. The complexity of today's publications requires more reliable and objective methods of making decisions. This is a problem that the professional press has just started to realize. Evaluation and feedback are means for improvement, not ends in themselves.

Chapter 14

ETC.

> It's not whether you win or lose,
> but how you write the game that
> counts.
>
> —FELDMAN'S LAW

This chapter will attempt to cover problems that are seldom mentioned in textbooks. The solutions may not meet your situation, but they may suggest answers or enable you to anticipate trouble areas.

During the summer the adviser should gather two complete sets of the newspaper and have them bound. One should go to the school library and the other become part of the room reference library. This helps cut down foot traffic during the year that is both annoying and time consuming. Students have a minimum amount of working time during a period, and having source material immediately at hand is an enormous aid. If your school, like many, uses a computer for name lists, ask the principal for a complete print-out of the student body, preferably by grades. Thus editors can check the spelling of all names. The room should be equipped with a phone (although it sometimes becomes an annoyance as well as a help) and at least six to ten typewriters, depending on your publication schedule. A football coach can't train a team with one football, and journalism classes can't do the job with one or two typewriters.

When students do have to leave the room to check a story, problems often begin. Depending on school policy, students should be allowed to do some legwork during class time. Press cards, signed by both you and the principal, should be issued to identify students on assignments. This also helps build morale, which will be discussed later. Another safeguard is a sign-out sheet on which students note time of departure and destination. This should be posted each week so you will know where a student is and also as a check against over-use of the privilege.

Several things can be done in the summer to help insure a successful publications program. Students who don't type should take typing in summer school. If beginning journalism is a prerequisite to staff membership, offer the beginning course in summer school. Seniors often have an elective but do not want to take beginning journalism. The summer course may also be helpful for incoming sophomores, transfer students, or talented writers who might try journalism on a summer basis.

Even more important are preschool meetings for staff orientation. These might be keyed to producing an edition for incoming students. The highlight of the orientation sessions should be a meeting with student leaders and administrators on editorial policy. The opening of school is too late and too hectic to hold background meetings. An overnight retreat, complete with professional editors as guest resource leaders, helps build the esprit de corps that is necessary for a successful year. Yearbook and newspaper staffs thus get to know many of their news sources, and the latter learn about publication problems.

STAFF MORALE

An adviser has to plan a full-year campaign to maintain staff morale at a high level. The retreat or orientation is an excellent ice-breaker that lends prestige to your program. The spacing of activities and rewards helps to stabilize morale during the long 36-week "season." Journalism days at the university and writing contests serve as boosts, but they are not enough. Field trips to newspaper offices and television stations, and interviews and press conferences with athletes, actors, school officials, or politicians are especially helpful in expanding the horizon of students. Field trips to magazine and engraving plants, radio stations, and offices of newsmen assigned to police, court, or governmental beats, and attending and reviewing community plays and concerts are often overlooked. Quill & Scroll club meetings with other schools often spark a program. One of the best second-semester projects is to have your regular staff work at the community daily while an edition is put out. Your entire staff is excused for the day to go out on assignment with professionals.

The smile on a student's face at an awards banquet is the climax that every journalism program needs. Parents and students suddenly realize the scope and importance of what many had previously felt was just another class.

This includes photographers, columnists, beat reporters, business and advertising representatives, and cartoonists. The size of the paper will dictate the number of students you can utilize, but even a small daily or weekly will cooperate.

If you can't take the students out, you can always bring visitors in. These press conferences, with each student writing a story and the best one appearing in the newspaper, can really help students learn to ask probing questions. Principals, coaches, professional journalists, and politicians are all fair game.

The highlight of the year, of course, should be the publications banquet. I feel that the newspaper, yearbook, literary magazine, and photography and printing departments deserve such a banquet. Awards should include certificates to all seniors plus pen sets or other appropriate recognition to key editors. Publishers usually can be persuaded to sponsor contests for yearly bests in news, sports, features, photos, and editorial writing. First-place cash awards up to $25 make for real competition among staff members, who may enter one story per category. The newspaper does the judging, and the publisher makes the awards at the banquet. Superintendent, principal, parents, and guest lecturers should be invited. Parents like to attend and will pay their own way, but students are sometimes hesitant about encouraging them to do so. Alumni also like to attend, particularly former editors, and such occasions as a 25th or 50th "birthday" of the publication are ideal for showcasing the banquet.

Gimmicks may not always be the answer, but they often provide the needed incentive for a staff to make an extra effort. Special editions are one way to do this. During National Newspaper Week we once turned out an extra edition on journalism that was used to recruit staff members. It was given to English classes, counselors, and junior-high publications staffs. Contests sponsored by insurance companies and patriotic organizations may warrant special stories or editions. Instead of the usual senior edition, one staff designed a magazine that covered the final weeks that escape the yearbook. Special sports editions that can be sold as game programs or souvenirs can often bring in needed revenue. One year the staff suggested sponsoring a beauty contest for a newspaper queen. This proved an excellent promotion and money-maker. Whenever possible, the activity should have something to do with journalism.

Many times the real problem is that the principal trims the publication budget with a hatchet and the adviser and staff have to expend time and energy raising funds instead of concentrating on journalism. If the budget is not realistic, the adviser and staff should negotiate with the student body and administration for additional funds. In this situation a publications board can be of immense value in adjudicating financial battles as well as editorial ones. Representation on this board should include staff, student body, faculty, and administration. The jurisdiction could include approval of editors, budget, editorial policy, and advertising rates.

SURVEY OF ADVISERS

One of the major problems in publications is the high turn-over rate of advisers. By the time advisers understand the legal and ethical issues of student journalism, they return to the comfort of the English classroom. In a survey[1] of 213 high-school and junior-high advisers in California, almost two-thirds (141) were in their first five years, and 83 did not intend to continue as advisers. There were more than three times as many advisers in their first five years as there were in the six-to-ten-year bracket, and four times as many in the 11-to-30-year bracket.

Some of the reasons for the high turnover may be found in teacher preparation. Only 16 of the 231 had majored in journalism, another six had a master's degree in communications, and 14 had minored in journalism. More than half of the 231 did not feel adequately trained as journalism teachers when first assigned the job. Can you imagine this happening in athletics! Some 78 had no training of any kind, 29 had five units or less of undergraduate training, and 28 had five or less units in graduate school. Only 23 had field or professional experience.

More than half of the schools reported that one teacher handled all publications in addition to the regular teaching load. Out of 231, only 85 received extra pay, one as low as $50 and two as high as $600. Thirty-five reported released time, which

[1] Dorothy McPhillips, "Orange County Journalism Education Survey," Spring, 1966.

104 preferred to extra pay. Among the problems cited frequently were large classes, financial troubles, inadequate physical conditions, and a shortage of good students.

The conclusions and recommendations of the report were as follows:

CONCLUSIONS

(1) Teacher turnover is caused by inadequate training, overloading, and unrealistic scheduling of teachers and students.

(2) If educational journalism in the secondary schools of California is to gain status, administrators will have to hire qualified advisers and see that they are not overloaded.

(3) There is a need for a definite educational program in the state for qualifying journalism teachers.

(4) A reasonable period of released time is recommended for publications advisers.

(5) It is unreasonable to expect a teacher to advise student publications and teach a beginning journalism class during the same period. It is equally unreasonable to expect a teacher to advise two student publications within the same period.

(6) There is a need for a common course of study adopted by the state for teachers and administrators to use as a standard.

RECOMMENDATIONS

(1) One period of released time is recommended for teachers advising the school newspaper and/or the yearbook in addition to the conference period for the regular teaching schedule.

(2) Investigations should be made in all areas of journalism to detect changes in practices and trends and to give recognition and support to those meeting high standards.

(3) Unusual and interest-producing journalism courses of study, and innovations in the teaching of journalism should be given recognition through publicity and honors.

(4) Recognition and honor should be given to journalism teachers and advisers who have devoted many years to the program.

(5) To assure better-trained publications advisers, the state should set stringent requirements for certification to teach journalism courses and/or advise student publications. Schools should be

given a time period within which to meet the educational requirements for an approved journalism program.

(6) A common course of study should be recommended to the state.

(7) A beginning journalism course of study should be adopted and recognized by the state and included as a specific subject in the curriculum.

(8) Professional organizations should make an effort to gain knowledge of the problems and unique peculiarities of high-school journalism. Five key problems involve time, scheduling, inability to get good students into the program, physical conditions and equipment, financial support, and inadequate teacher training.

(9) A request should be made to professional organizations to support and publicize these recommendations.

Exceptions to the high turnover rate are not many, but they do convey some of the reasons for survival. One teacher, after more than three decades as an adviser to highly successful publications, made these comments:

As a journalism teacher I don't have to *pose* as an eccentric; people accept me as such, but I bask in the realization that I have sent my staff members out into the community with a finer understanding of it, and a better understanding of their school because as journalists they have been an integral part of it (perhaps even more so than many faculty members). I smile serenely over the family feeling of rapport within my staff and know they are better prepared for group work. I have seen the silent ones become articulate, and the numb ones, intense and vocal through the interplay of ideas in the classroom.

I decide to "keep the book" or "have the paper." After all, I have lived through it when the *Last of the Mohicans* came out as the *Lust of the Mohicans*. I learned to control the smutty, the filthy, the lies, and the gossip column instincts. I have been able to make writers realize that though postal regulations forbid obscenity, and like laws cover matters of character, they, as writers, must always depend upon their own good taste and sense of fair play to keep the magic of the printed word from becoming black magic.

Of course, I'm willing to try another year because I enjoyed taking my students on trips to printing plants, to museums, libraries, art exhibits, and the theater. I have made them realize that a Broadway play, to be successful, is more than a Kinsey report with gestures, and regardless of new trends in art or cars, they learned that standards of good writing remain amazingly stable, dependable, and meaningful in an otherwise chaotic world.

In a day when "managed news" is on everyone's tongue, the journalism classroom becomes the finest laboratory for clinical research, soul research, word research, and story research for anything that is slanted, suppressed, or colored. Student journalists learn to know that the sins of omission in writing may be more deadly than those of commission, and that there are no disputes about facts— only ignorance.

Journalism, the handmaiden of democracy, has been my weapon, inspiration, and goal while trying to convince youth that in order to write for our way of living, they must become intimately acquainted with the social, economic and political experiences around them— and oppose selfish and unwholesome interests.[1]

LEGAL SAFEGUARDS

School publications, like professional newspapers, have no peculiar privilege, but are liable for what they publish. One safeguard for advisers and school boards is liability insurance. In some states laws make it mandatory to carry such insurance. Another safeguard is good judgment. Negligence has been one of the key words in suits against school districts. This means that the awarding of damages may hinge on the ability to prove negligence on the part of the adviser.

A recent ruling in California, in reviewing liability for improper supervision, commented:

It was a jury question where proper supervision would . . . have prevented the accident. If the jury should find that . . . [the] injury was of the same general type likely to occur in the absence of safeguards, [the] intervening act [of the student] would be no more than a concurring cause. School authorities have a duty to supervise, at

[1] Christina D. Beeson, "Journalism, a Pragmatic Approach to Democracy," *Journal of Secondary Education,* November 1963.

all times, the conduct of children on the school grounds. A school district may thus be liable for failure of its officers or employees to use the ordinary care in this respect. It is not necessary to prove that the very injuries which occurred must have been foreseeable, merely that a reasonably prudent person would foresee that injuries of the same general type would be likely to occur in the absence of adequate safeguards. . . .[1]

The strongest statement dismissing the danger of libel suits comes from Robert C. Boffa:

It appears obvious that in the overwhelming number of situations a public institution faces no real threat of liability for the torts which may result from student press activities. The successive barriers of state sovereign immunity, immunity from tort liability, and general nonliability for acts of students render unconvincing the argument that the student press must be controlled in order to save the state from liability. Both the attitude and the acts of the legislative and judicial branches seem to afford adequate safeguards against liability.[2]

Although Boffa's conclusions may have seemed safe when they were made, such settlements as in the Bickerton case point to new interpretations. The courts are now in sympathy with the individual, and the immunity of the state to suits has been shattered in many states. The perils of publishing seem to be increasing in this litigation-minded era.

ETHICAL SAFEGUARDS

As has been seen, lack of journalism training hampers supervision of student publications. The new and often insecure adviser allows poor conditions to exist because of ignorance, concern for job security, and hope that a quiet tenure will lead to a

---

[1] Ziegler vs. Santa Cruz City High School District, 162 Cal. App. 2 777, 284, 335 P. 2 709 (1959).

[2] Robert C. Boffa, "A Study of the Liability of a State Education Institution for the Torts of Its Student Press." Philadelphia: United States National Student Association, 1961.

quicker escape. A strong publications board with written policies, cooperation with other extracurricular sponsors to insure adequate extra pay, individual efforts to secure needed courses and methods, and up-to-date instruction of an emerging discipline are needed to insure professional standards in scholastic journalism. Administrators, who often think of publications only as tools of public relations, must not place the weakest, newest English teacher in charge of such an important part of student life. Ethically, as well as legally, the school stands *in loco parentis,* with powers over students similar to those held by a parent over his children. Student publications have no legal grounds to demand editorial freedom, but there is strong ethical and moral backing for limited freedom. Understanding of the adolescent aids in recognizing his need for such freedom. The teen-ager wants to be independent and prove he can think for himself. One way to do this is by attacking the standards of the Establishment, rebelling against authority. During this difficult period, the student needs freedom to help declare his independence and individuality and also controls to protect him from editorial excesses. Publications offer both freedom and restraint and an opportunity for the student journalist to solve his own legal and ethical problems.

Appendix A

THE JOURNALIST'S CREED

I Believe in the Profession of Journalism.

I believe that the public journal is a public trust; that all connected with it are, to the full measure of their responsibility, trustees for the public; that acceptance of a lesser service than the public service is betrayal of this trust.

I believe that clear thinking and clear statement, accuracy, and fairness, are fundamental to good journalism.

I believe that a journalist should write only what he holds in his heart to be true.

I believe that suppression of the news, for any consideration other than the welfare of society, is indefensible.

I believe that no one should write as a journalist what he would not say as a gentleman; that bribery by one's own pocketbook is as much to be avoided as bribery by the pocketbook of another; that individual responsibility may not be escaped by pleading another's instructions or another's dividends.

I believe that advertising, news and editorial columns should alike serve the best interests of readers; that a single standard of helpful truth and cleanness should prevail for all; that the supreme test of good journalism is the measure of its public service.

I believe that the journalism which succeeds best—and best deserves success—fears God and honors man; is stoutly independent, unmoved by pride of opinion or greed of power, constructive, tolerant but never careless, self-controlled, patient, always respectful of its readers but always unafraid; is quickly indignant at injustice; is unswayed by the appeal of privilege or the clamor of the mob; seeks to give every man

169

a chance, and, as far as law and honest wage and recognition of human brotherhood can make it so, an equal chance; is profoundly patriotic while sincerely promoting international good will and cementing world-comradeship; is a journalism of humanity, of and for today's world.

Walter Williams

DEAN, SCHOOL OF JOURNALISM, UNIVERSITY OF MISSOURI, 1908–1935

Appendix B

CANONS OF JOURNALISM

The American Society of Newspaper Editors on April 28, 1923, adopted a set of ethical rules to be followed by its members. Although some newspapers do not practice these rules, the rules remain sound canons and just aspirations of American journalism.

Canons of Journalism

A. Responsibility

The right of a newspaper to attract and hold readers is restricted by nothing but consideration of public welfare. The use a newspaper makes of the share of public attention it gains serves to determine its sense of responsibility, which it shares with every member of its staff. A journalist who uses his power for any selfish or otherwise unworthy purpose is faithless to a high trust.

B. Freedom of the Press

Freedom of the press is to be guarded as a vital right of mankind. It is the unquestionable right to discuss whatever is not explicitly forbidden by law, including the wisdom of any restrictive statute. To its privileges under the freedom of American institutions are inseparably joined its responsibilities for an intelligent fidelity to the Constitution of the United States.

C. Independence

Freedom from all obligations except that of fidelity to the public interest is vital. Promotion of any private interest contrary to the general welfare, for whatever reason, is not compatible with honest journalism. So-called news communications from private sources should not be published without public notice of their source or else substantiation of their claims to value as news, both in form and substance. Partisanship in editorial comment which knowingly departs from the truth does violence to the best spirit of American journalism; in the news columns it is subversive of a fundamental principle of the profession.

D. Sincerity, Truthfulness, Accuracy

Good faith with the reader is the foundation of all journalism worthy of the name. By every consideration of good faith, a newspaper is constrained to be truthful. It is not to be excused for lack of thoroughness, or accuracy within its control, or failure to obtain command of these essential qualities.

Headlines should be fully warranted by the contents of the articles which they surmount.

E. Impartiality

Sound practice makes clear distinction between news reports and expressions of opinion. News reports should be free from opinion or bias of any kind. This rule does not apply to so-called special articles unmistakably devoted to advocacy or characterized by a signature authorizing the writer's own conclusions and interpretations.

F. Fair Play

1. A newspaper should not publish unofficial charges affecting reputation or moral character, without giving the accused an opportunity to be heard; right practice demands the giving of such opportunity in all cases of serious accusations outside judicial proceedings.

2. A newspaper should not invade the rights of private feelings without sure warrant of public right as distinguished from public curiosity.

3. It is the privilege, as it is the duty, of a newspaper to make prompt and complete correction of its own serious mistakes of fact or opinion, whatever their origin.

G. Decency

A newspaper cannot escape conviction of insincerity if, while professing high moral purpose, it supplies incentives to base conduct, such as are to be found in details of crime and vice, publication of which is not demonstrably for the general good. Lacking authority to enforce its canons, the journalism here represented can but express the hope that deliberate pandering to vicious instincts will encounter effective public disapproval or yield to the influence of a preponderant professional condemnation.

Appendix C

PRESS CRITICISM [1]

A. Unreliability

1. Because of the speed with which reporting must be done and the fact that human beings are doing the reporting, inaccuracies sometimes occur. These errors are never condoned by reputable newspapers, however.

2. All newspapers strive to verify beyond any possibility of doubt all the news that they publish.

3. Sometimes, of course, newspapers cannot be sure of the authenticity of their news reports. When they cannot be certain, they often indicate the sources from which the news was obtained and leave to the reader's judgment what to believe. Common in World War II, when some news was particularly hard to verify, were such expressions as "according to an official American communique" or "information released by an English censor."

4. Information that comes from open, revealed sources is probably true. When the source is hidden or obscure, you should be careful what you believe.

5. The degree to which a newspaper departs from objective reporting, even though through byline stories, the more the opportunity for misuse of news columns increases.

    a. Pernicious propaganda and malicious suggestion can masquerade as comment.

    b. Crimes against society, not to mention misdemeanors, can be committed in the name of Interpretation as well as of Liberty.

    c. News may be colored to further a cause either good or bad.

[1] Adapted from *Editing the Day's News*, 3rd Ed., George C. Bastian and Leland D. Case. The Macmillan Co.

B. Superficialities

1. As the educational levels of newspaper readers rise, the content of newspapers changes.
    a. Newspapers with a majority of well-educated readers have few, if any, cheap, scandalous news stories and features.
    b. Newspapers with a majority of poorly educated readers have fewer meaningful, thought-provoking articles.

2. Because of the increase in the number of well-educated people, newspaper interests are changing. Newspapers now publish book reviews, art and theater columns, and news of science, church, financial activities.

3. Newspaper readers themselves have much to do with the charge of superficiality in the daily press.

4. News of significance can be made readable to a majority of people by wise editors and well-trained reporters.

C. Sensationalism

1. Some news is naturally sensational. To fulfill its duty of publishing the news, a newspaper must print these stories.

2. Some critics who charge sensationalism ordinarily do not object to the publication of sensational news. They do object, however, to playing up these stories beyond their true news value. They object, also, to the inclusion in crime stories of all the horrible details. They charge that such details have a bad effect on the mentally and socially weak and on youth whose emotions have not yet become stable.

3. Other critics say that the publication and big display of crime stories give newspapers "an opportunity to direct popular attention to the facts of scientific criminology. Details of a juvenile delinquency case can be made a springboard for a report on what the community is doing, or should do, to prevent such things happening again. All the horror aroused by a gruesome murder can be canalized to an understanding of why it was committed and the ways society can prevent other murders. . . . Frank and detailed crime reporting, it is reasoned, is in itself a deterrent to crime—especially if the police and courts do their work properly so that it can be climaxed with an account of the law's retribution."

D. Personal privacy

1. A few newspapers, perhaps, do not respect "the inalienable right of the individual to privacy."

2. Publishing a picture portraying a mother's grief at the grave of her son is probably not in the realm of good taste.

3. There are times and situations when the expression "nobody's business" applies.

4. Prominent people may be bothered more than are common, ordinary people, by newsmen in moments that should be private.

E. Obstructing justice

1. Critics occasionally comment, "The case was tried in the newspapers."

2. Newspapers do publish stories of cases being tried in courts and sometimes even offer opinions on cases before a decision has been reached.

    a. Lawyers and judges often object to the newspaper discussion of these court cases before verdicts are returned because they say that such discussion interferes with their ability to obtain a jury, to secure unbiased testimony from witnesses, and generally to conduct a fair trial.

    b. Contempt of court citations have been used as a weapon against newspapers who "try" cases in the public press. Reporters argue, however, that they are within their legal right of free speech when expressing such opinions.

    c. Courts have upheld that newspapers are well within their rights to criticize the decisions of judges and juries *after* cases have been closed.

3. Although newspapers sometimes hinder justice in their eagerness to be first with the news, few newspapers would knowingly obstruct the courts in giving persons fair trials.

CRITERIA FOR A GOOD NEWSPAPER

The criteria committee of the Associated Press Managing Editors Association drew up this definition and these criteria for a good newspaper:

A good newspaper prints the important news and provides information, comment and guidance which are most useful to its readers.

It reports fully and explains the meaning of local, national, and international events which are of major significance in its own community. Its editorial comment provides an informed opinion on matters of vital concern to its readers.

By reflecting the total image of its own community in its news coverage and by providing wise counsel in its editorials, a good newspaper becomes a public conscience. It also must be lively, imaginative and original; it must have a sense of humor, and the power to arouse keen interest.

To implement these principles of good editing requires a skilled staff, an attractive format, adequate space for news and comment, and a sound business foundation.

The staff must possess the professional pride and competence necessary to breathe life and meaning into the daily record of history. Good writing must be combined with an effective typographical display of copy and pictures to capture the full drama and excitement of the day's news. Good printing is essential.

News and comment of most immediate interest and importance to the local community shall have priority for the available space, which will depend on the size and resources of the newspaper.

To assure a financially strong and independent publication, and one that is competitive with other media, a good newspaper must maintain effective circulation, advertising, and promotion departments.

Criteria of a Good Newspaper

A good newspaper may judge its own performance—and be judged —by the criteria which follow:

ACCURACY—The newspaper shall:
1. Exert maximum effort to print the truth in all news statements.
2. Strive for completeness and objectivity.
3. Guard against carelessness, bias, or distortion by either emphasis or omission.

RESPONSIBILITY—The newspaper shall:
1. Use mature and considered judgment in the public interest at all times.
2. Select, edit, and display news on the basis of the significance and its genuine usefulness to the public.
3. Edit news affecting public morals with candor and good taste and avoid an imbalance of sensational, preponderantly negative, or merely trivial news.
4. Accent when possible a reasonable amount of news which illustrates the values of compassion, self-sacrifice, heroism, good citizenship, and patriotism.
5. Clearly define sources of news, and tell the reader when competent sources cannot be identified.
6. Respect rights of privacy.
7. Instruct its staff members to conduct themselves with dignity and decorum.

INTEGRITY—The newspaper shall:
1. Maintain vigorous standards of honesty and fair play in the selection and editing of its contents as well as in all relations with news sources and the public.
2. Deal dispassionately with controversial subjects and treat disputed issues with impartiality.
3. Practice humility and tolerance in the face of honest conflicting opinions or disagreement.
4. Provide a forum for the exchange of pertinent comment and

criticism, especially if it is in conflict with the newspaper's editorial point of view.

5. Label its own editorial views or expressions of opinion

LEADERSHIP—The newspaper shall:

1. Act with courage in serving the public.
2. Stimulate and vigorously support public officials, private groups, and individuals in crusades and campaigns to increase the good works and eliminate the bad in the community.
3. Help to protect all rights and privileges guaranteed by law.
4. Serve as a constructive critic of government at all levels, providing leadership for necessary reforms or innovations, and exposing any misfeasance in office or any misuse of public power.
5. Oppose demagogues and other selfish and unwholesome interests regardless of their size or influence.

Guide for a Good Newspaper

A good newspaper should be guided in the publication of all material by a concern for truth, the hallmark of freedom, by a concern for human decency and human betterment, and by a respect for the accepted standards of its own community.

Appendix E

STATEMENT OF PRINCIPLES
OF THE UNITED STATES STUDENT
PRESS ASSOCIATION [1]

ARTICLE I. Whereas the United States Student Press Association believes the following principles:

1. That freedom of expression and debate by means of a free and vigorous press is essential to the effectiveness of an educational community in a democratic society;

2. That where the student press is a function to the student government, or of the university administration, this should in no way be allowed to impair the freedom of the student press;

3. That the student press should be free of all forms of external interference;

4. That it is essential to a free student press that it be responsible for the views and opinions that it expresses;

5. That the basic duties of such a free student press are to present the various opinions of the students it represents, to present news fairly and without bias, to interpret local, national and international events, and issues of interest and import to students to the best of its ability;

ARTICLE II. And whereas freedom of the student press has been abridged in the following ways:

1. Confiscation of issues of student newspapers due to the publication of material which faculty or administration authorities con-

[1] SOURCE: The United States Student Press Association, 3457 Chestnut Street, Philadelphia, Pennsylvania.

180

sidered detrimental to the reputation and welfare of the institution, or some department of the institution;

2. Suspension, expulsion, or threat of similar action against student editor;

3. Suspension, or threatened suspension of publications because the publishing or proposed publishing of matters which faculty, or administrative authorities considered detrimental to the reputation and welfare of the institution, or some department of the institution;

4. Control of the content of a student newspaper through censorship by faculty, administrative authorities, and the student government so that the student newspaper tended to become a public relations organ of the institution or an instrument of the student government;

5. Financial pressure used to limit or retaliate against editorial policy;

6. By censorship of articles and/or editorial comment, by civil and academic authorities; and,

7. By inordinate and excessive pressure used to prevent publication of particular issues or opinions;

ARTICLE III. Therefore the United States Student Press Association affirms its belief that it should be free from abuses listed under Article II, and declares the following fundamental rights, duties, and responsibilities necessary for the effective implementation for the principles of Article I:

1. That the United States student press should be free from pressure by student governments, university authorities, or by any other external agencies;

2. That within the restrictions of the laws of libel and within the scope of their responsibilities and duties as outlined in Article I, the United States student press should be autonomous; and,

3. That the United States student press should be free to develop so that it can continue to fulfill its role in the academic community.

Appendix F

STATEMENT OF PRINCIPLES CONCERNING THE STUDENT PRESS BY THE AMERICAN CIVIL LIBERTIES UNION [1]

A. Freedom of Expression

"The student government, student organizations, and individual students should be free to discuss, and to pass resolutions, distribute leaflets, circulate petitions, and take other lawful action respecting any matter which directly or indirectly concerns or affects them.

"Students should take responsibility for helping to maintain a free academic community. They should respect and defend not only their fellow students' freedoms; but also their teachers' right to the free expression of views based on their own pursuit of the truth and their right to function as citizens, independent of the college or university."

. . . .

E. Student Publications

All student publications—college newspapers, literary and humor magazines, academic periodicals and yearbooks—should enjoy full freedom of the press. They are too often denied it by college administrations which fear public criticism. Except for the relatively few university dailies which are independent financially, college publications in general are dependent on the administration's favor in that they use campus facilities and are subsidized either directly by the college or indirectly by a tax on student funds.

The college newspaper: Whether a daily or a weekly, the campus paper should report news of student interest on and off campus, should provide an outlet for student and faculty opinion through

[1] SOURCE: American Civil Liberties Union. "Academic Freedom and Civil Liberties of Students in Colleges and Universities," *AAUP Bulletin*, Vol. 48 (June 1962), pp. 110–115.

letters to the editor, and make its own editorial comments on college and other matters. While these comments need not necessarily represent the view of the majority of students, fair space should be given to dissenting opinion.

The advisory board of the college newspaper, or college publications board which supervises all student publications, should be composed of at least a majority of students, selected by the student government or council or by some other democratic method. Other members might include a member of the faculty of the School of Journalism in universities with such schools, an alumnus, a local newspaper editor, or other qualified citizen, and such representation from the liberal arts faculty and/or Dean's office as may be mutually agreed upon.

One of the main duties of the publications or advisory board may be the interviewing of qualified candidates and the selection of the editor-in-chief and possibly of all the major staff writers on the campus newspaper. In colleges where this is not the practice, some other method of selection appropriate to the institution should be devised by the student government to ensure that competent responsible editors are put in charge and that the college newspaper does not fall into the hands of a self-perpetuating clique.

The editor-in-chief should be left free to exercise his own best judgment in the selection of material to be published. The adults on the board (or the faculty adviser if the paper has a single consultant) should counsel the editors in the ethics and responsibilities of journalism, but neither a faculty member nor an administrator should exercise veto power over what may be printed. Should the board as a whole, after publication, consider that the paper's editor has exercised poor judgment, in one or a number of instances, it may take steps to impeach and remove him from office after holding hearings and according him due process rights.

Appendix G

SAMPLE BOARD OF PUBLICATIONS BY-LAWS:
THE DAILY CALIFORNIAN
University of California, Berkeley

Daily Californian Publisher's Board

I. Membership: There shall be fourteen (14) voting members and two (2) non-voting members of the Board.

A. The Voting Members shall be:

6 students:
    1 ASUC President
    4 students-at-large selected by the Publisher's Board and approved by the ASUC Senate. These students shall have at least junior standing during their entire term of office. One of these students may be a graduate.
    1 graduate council president

3 faculty:
    1 Journalism professor appointed by the Academic Senate
    1 Business Administration professor appointed by the Academic Senate
    1 Law professor appointed by the Faculty of the School Law

3 administration appointed by the Chancellor:
    1 Public Information Officer
    1 Member, Dean of Students Office
    1 at-large

2 professional journalists appointed by the Chancellor and approved by the ASUC Senate.

B. The Non-voting Members shall be:

1 *Daily Cal* Editor
1 *Daily Cal* Business Manager

C. Term of Office:

1. Student members shall serve for one (1) year. Two of the students-at-large shall be appointed in the spring, two in the fall. (This will necessitate two of the initial appointments serving for only six months.)

2. All other voting members shall serve for three (3) years with the exception of the initial occupants of these positions.

> The first Journalism professor shall serve for one (1) year. The first Business Administration professor shall serve for two (2) years. The first Law professor shall serve for three (3) years. The first at-large administration representative shall serve for one (1) year. The first Public Information Officer shall serve for two (2) years. The first member of the Dean of Students Office shall serve for three (3) years. One professional journalist shall serve for two (2) years, the other for three (3) years.

II. Meetings and Quorum:

The Publisher's Board shall meet once a week while school is in session. Additional meetings may be called by the Chairman or a majority of the Board. A quorum shall consist of eight (8) voting members of the Board.

III. Functions and Powers of the Board:

A. This body shall be the publisher of the *Daily Californian*.

B. The Board possesses final authority of appointment. The Board may remove for stated cause after hearing by vote of at least 2/3 of the voting members any such appointments. Such hearings shall be public if so requested by the person being considered for removal.

    C. The Board shall not possess the power of prior censorship.

    D. The Board will elect its own chairman in the fall of each year for one year. The Chairman shall be a student member of the Board.

    E. These by-laws shall be amended by a two-thirds (2/3) majority of the Board subject to approval by the ASUC Senate.

    F. This body shall receive and evaluate all complaints and suggestions regarding *Daily Californian* coverage and policy and take the appropriate action.